TEACHER'S GUIDE

GRADE 2

READING AND WRITING Sourcebook

Authors

Ruth Nathan
Laura Robb

Great Source Education Group

a division of Houghton Mifflin Company
Wilmington, Massachusetts
www.greatsource.com

Authors

Ruth Nathan, one of the authors of *Writers Express, Write on Track,* and *Write Away,* is the author of many professional books and articles on literacy. She earned a Ph.D. in reading from Oakland University in Rochester, Michigan, where she co-headed their reading research laboratory for several years. She currently teaches the third grade and consults with numerous schools and organizations on reading. Ms. Nathan recently spoke in front of the U.S. Senate on the topic of best practices.

Laura Robb, author of *Reading Strategies That Work; Summer Success: Reading; Literacy Links; Teaching Reading in Social Studies, Science, and Math;* and *Teaching Reading in the Middle School,* has taught language arts at Powhatan School in Boyce, Virginia, for more than 30 years. She also mentors and coaches teachers in Virginia public schools and speaks at conferences throughout the country.

Printed in the United States of America.

International Standard Book Number: 0-669-50804-7

2 3 4 5 6 7 8 9 10—P00—09 08 07 06 05

Readers and Reviewers

Judith Aiken
North Londonderry Elementary
Londonderry, NH

Madeline Andrews
North Londonderry Elementary
Londonderry, NH

Ellen Barker
Patronis Elementary School
Panama City Beach, FL

Heather Beach
Bethany Elementary School
Beaverton, OR

Nancy Brown
Bethany Elementary School
Beaverton, OR

Barbara Clemons
Patronis Elementary School
Panama City Beach, FL

Marilyn Crow
Wilmette Public Schools
Wilmette, IL

Maureen Grant
Sunnyside Elementary School
Arden Hills, MN

Kathleen Keating
Valentine Hills Elementary School
Arden Hills, MN

Jamie Kelly
Patronis Elementary School
Panama City Beach, FL

Carolyn Kreibich
Turtle Lake Elementary
Shoreview, MN

Jeanette Nichols
Dixon School
Chicago, IL

Betsy Smith
Santa Rosa, CA

Laura Tolone
Grand Prairie Elementary
Frankfort, IL

Katrina Watters
Santa Rita School
Los Altos, CA

Jeanne Woods
Bethany Elementary School
Beaverton, OR

Table of Contents

Table of Contents

Lesson Resources

PUPIL'S EDITION SKILLS AND STRATEGIES

The chart below identifies the strategies for each part of each pupil's lesson.

Selection	I. Prereading	II. Response Notes	Comprehension
1. *I Am an Apple* (nonfiction)	predict and preview	retell	draw
2. *Mice Squeak, We Speak* (nonfiction)	preview	question	draw
3. *Bread, Bread, Bread* (nonfiction)	K-W-L chart	connect	web
4. "Sam's Story" (fiction)	word web	draw	retell
5. *Shoes, Shoes, Shoes* (nonfiction)	preview	question	visualize
6. *Building a House* (nonfiction)	predict and preview	mark	retell
7. *Water* (nonfiction)	anticipation guide	draw	explain
8. *Too Many Rabbits* (fiction)	predict	connect	sequence
9. *Ronald Morgan Goes to Bat* (fiction)	preview	question	retell
10. *The Golly Sisters Go West* (fiction)	predict and preview	draw	sequence
11. *Stars* (nonfiction)	anticipation guide	question	explain
12. *Duckling Days* (fiction)	predict and preview	connect	sequence
13. *Clean Your Room, Harvey Moon!* (poetry)	word web	explain	retell
14. *Wilhe'mina Miles After the Stork Night* (fiction)	preview	question	explain

Word Work (phonics)	Word Work (structure)	III. Writing	Grammar/Usage
short *a*	suffixes	sentence	initial capitalization
short *u*	plurals	sentence	end punctuation
short *a*	*y* endings	sentence	complete sentence
short *o*	suffixes	sentences	initial capitalization
short vowels	plurals	sentences	end punctuation
short *i*	compound words	sentences	complete sentence
long *i*	syllables	paragraph	paragraph indents
long *e*	plurals	narrative paragraph	paragraph indents
long *o*	compound words	journal entry	end punctuation
long *a*	suffixes	note/message	capitalization; commas
long *i*	homophones	descriptive paragraph	complete sentences
short vowels	suffixes	narrative paragraph	paragraph indents
long vowel review	contractions	poem	apostrophes
long and short vowels	syllables	friendly letter	capitalization; commas

TEACHER'S GUIDE SKILLS AND STRATEGIES

The chart below identifies the strategies for each part of each Teacher's Guide lesson.

Selection	Vocabulary	Prereading	Comprehension
1. *I Am an Apple* (nonfiction)	vocabulary strategies	predict and preview	stop and explain
2. *Mice Squeak, We Speak* (nonfiction)	context clues	preview	draw
3. *Bread, Bread, Bread* (nonfiction)	predict and go	K-W-L chart	connect
4. "*Sam's Story*" (fiction)	context clues	word web	retell
5. *Shoes, Shoes, Shoes* (nonfiction)	plurals	preview	visualize
6. *Building a House* (nonfiction)	context clues	predict and preview	retell
7. *Water* (nonfiction)	context clues	anticipation guide	explain
8. *Too Many Rabbits* (fiction)	plurals	predict	connect
9. *Ronald Morgan Goes to Bat* (fiction)	past tense	preview	retell
10. *The Golly Sisters Go West* (fiction)	silent letters	predict and preview	retell
11. *Stars* (nonfiction)	antonyms	anticipation guide	question
12. *Duckling Days* (fiction)	*r*-controlled vowels	predict and preview	connect
13. *Clean Your Room, Harvey Moon!* (poetry)	syllables	word web	retell
14. *Wilhe'mina Miles After the Stork Night* (fiction)	suffixes	preview	explain

Word Work	Word Work	Writing	Assessment
short *a*	suffixes	sentence	multiple-choice test
short *u*	plurals	sentence	multiple-choice test
short *a*	*y* endings	sentence	multiple-choice test
short *o*	suffixes	two sentences	multiple-choice test
short vowels	plurals	three sentences	multiple-choice test
short *i*	compound words	three sentences	multiple-choice test
long *i*	syllables	paragraph	multiple-choice test
long *e*	plurals	narrative paragraph	multiple-choice test
long *o*	compound words	journal entry	multiple-choice test
long *a*	suffixes	note/message	multiple-choice test
long *i*	homophones	descriptive paragraph	multiple-choice test
short vowels	suffixes	narrative paragraph	multiple-choice test
long vowel review	contractions	poem	multiple-choice test
long and short vowels	dividing words	friendly letter	multiple-choice test

CORRELATION TO *WRITE ONE* AND *WRITE AWAY*

Like the *Write One* and *Write Away* handbooks, the *Sourcebook* will appeal to teachers who believe that writing is a way of learning. This *Sourcebook*, like *Write Away*, is a book to "grow in." Here students read a series of carefully sequenced selections and respond to them. They jot notes, create organizers, plan and brainstorm compositions, and write drafts of their work. The *Sourcebook* is one way for students to read and write weekly, if not daily.

In the *Sourcebooks*, both the kinds of writing and the lessons on Grammar, Usage, and Mechanics afford the best opportunities to use the *Write One* or *Write Away* handbooks as a reference. To make this convenient, the writing activities are correlated to the handbooks below, and the Grammar, Usage, and Mechanics lessons are correlated on the following page.

For Writing

Selection Title	Writing Activity	*Write One* ©2002 (pages)	*Write Away* ©2002 (pages)
1. *I Am an Apple*	sentence	28–29	51–55
2. *Mice Squeak, We Speak*	sentence	28–29	51–55
3. *Bread, Bread, Bread*	sentence	28–29	51–55
4. *"Sam's Story"*	sentences	28–29	51–55
5. *Shoes, Shoes, Shoes*	sentences	28–29	51–55
6. *Building a House*	sentences	28–29	51–55
7. *Water*	paragraph	50–53	56–63
8. *Too Many Rabbits*	narrative paragraph	50–53	61
9. *Ronald Morgan Goes to Bat*	journal entry	38–39	65–67
10. *The Golly Sisters Go West*	note/message	42–43	68–71
11. *Stars*	descriptive paragraph	50–53	58–59
12. *Duckling Days*	narrative paragraph	50–53	61
13. *Clean Your Room, Harvey Moon!*	poem	74–77	143–159
14. *Wilhe'mina Miles After the Stork Night*	friendly letter	44	72–75

CORRELATION TO *WRITE ONE* AND *WRITE AWAY*
For Grammar, Usage, and Mechanics

Selection Title	Grammar, Usage, and Mechanics	*Write One* ©*2002* (pages)	*Write Away* ©*2002* (pages)
1. *I Am an Apple*	initial capitalization	257	28, 30
2. *Mice Squeak, We Speak*	end punctuation	250–251	28–29, 32
3. *Bread, Bread, Bread*	complete sentence	51–52	28
4. *"Sam's Story"*	initial capitalization	257	28, 30
5. *Shoes, Shoes, Shoes*	end punctuation	250–251	28–29, 32
6. *Building a House*	complete sentence	51–52	28
7. *Water*	paragraph indents	60	50
8. *Too Many Rabbits*	paragraph indents	60	50
9. *Ronald Morgan Goes to Bat*	end punctuation	250–251	28–29, 32
10. *The Golly Sisters Go West*	capitalization; commas	252–253, 257–258	28, 30, 33
11. *Stars*	complete sentences	51–52	28
12. *Duckling Days*	paragraph indents	60	50
13. *Clean Your Room, Harvey Moon!*	apostrophes	254	33
14. *Wilhe'mina Miles After the Stork Night*	capitalization; commas	252–253, 257–258	28, 30, 33

OVERVIEW

This *Sourcebook* targets struggling readers. In Grade 2, these students need to be matched with quality literature that they can actually read. They need to be motivated, and they need good instruction in strategies that will help them learn how to transform a mass of words and lines into a comprehensible text. They also need help with getting ready to write; help with grammar, usage, and mechanics; and help with writing different kinds of texts—letters, journal entries, paragraphs, and so forth.

A Comprehensive Approach

Because struggling readers have so many different needs, they often receive a number of small, separate activities—work on main idea and details, a list of spelling rules, some word work on prefixes, practice writing a topic sentence, and review of spelling rules and comma rules. But it seldom adds up to a coherent whole for students.

That's where this *Sourcebook* comes in. The *Sourcebook* takes a holistic approach, not a piecemeal one. Through a comprehensive three-part lesson, each *Sourcebook* lesson walks students through the steps needed to read a text at their reading level and write about it. The lessons pull it all together for students, weaving together many different skills into a coherent whole.

The three-part lesson plan is:

I. BEFORE YOU READ (prereading)

II. READ (active reading, comprehending, and responding to literature)

III. WRITE (writing, revising, grammar, usage, and mechanics)

With this comprehensive approach, students can see the whole process of reading and writing. By following a consistent pattern, students can internalize the steps in the reading and the writing process. These patterns will help students build the habits they need to become successful readers and writers. See also the Overviews of book and lesson organization on pages 18–21.

A Strategy-Intensive Approach

The *Sourcebook* also is a strategy-intensive approach. Each *Sourcebook* builds students' repertoire of reading strategies in at least two areas:

1. To build motivation and background, prereading strategies are used to get students ready to read and to help them see the prior knowledge they already bring to their reading experiences.

2. To build comprehension, each *Sourcebook* uses three to five different comprehension strategies, such as webs, retelling, graphic organizers, and so on. By embedding these strategies in the literature, the *Sourcebook* shows students exactly which strategies to use and when to use them, building the habits of good readers. Then, after students finish reading, they are directed to go back and reread.

A Literature-Based Approach

Above all, the *Sourcebook* takes a literature-based approach. It presents 14 selections of quality literature of various genres by a wide range of authors. These selections are leveled in difficulty, starting with the easiest selection and progressing to more difficult ones. This leveling of the selections makes it easy to match students to literature they can actually read.

An Interactive Approach

The *Sourcebook* is an interactive book. It is intended to be a journal for students, in which they can write out their ideas about selections, plan and write out compositions, and record their progress throughout the year. Students should "own" their *Sourcebooks*, carrying them, reading in them, marking in them, and writing in them. They should become a record of their progress and accomplishments. Students will take pride in "their" *Sourcebook*.

Lesson Planning

A single *Sourcebook* lesson can be taught in approximately eight to ten class periods, whether that is over two or even three weeks.

DAY 1 Build background and discuss the selection.

DAY 2 Read the introduction. Do the prereading activities.

DAY 3 Introduce the selection. Discuss how to respond to the selection and the example. Then read the selection the first time.

DAY 4 Finish reading the selection. Then encourage students to read the selection again, this time writing in the Response Notes.

DAY 5 Finish reading. Reread the selection again, as necessary, and respond to the comprehension activities in the selection.

DAY 6 Do the Word Work that relates to phonics.

DAY 7 Do the Word Work activity that relates to word structure.

DAY 8 Begin the Writing Activity.

DAY 9 Finish writing. Talk about usage issues, and revise writing.

DAY 10 Reflect on the selection and what was learned.

Assessment

Each *Sourcebook* lesson includes a multiple-choice test for assessment, which is a useful gauge of student progress. Teachers need to demonstrate the progress their students have made throughout the year. The best measure of that progress will be a student's marked-up *Sourcebook* and the greater confidence and fluency with which students will be reading by the end of the year. For additional assessment ideas, see the **Strategy Handbook** in this *Teacher's Guide*.

MATCHING READERS WITH SELECTIONS

Probably one of the greatest challenges nowadays for teachers is matching readers with the right texts. The range of reading abilities in classrooms often spans four or even five grade levels. Some students read two grade levels below, and some read two or more grade levels above grade level. The teacher's job is to match each of his or her students (usually 25 to 35 children) to the exact right reading level, day in and day out. It is a large order.

What Level Is It?

To help match students to the appropriate books, we have relied on "readability formulas" and levels. None of these measures is perfectly reliable. They are crucial, however, because you cannot read every book before matching it to each student in class.

The solution adopted in the *Sourcebooks* for Grades 2–5 has been to begin with selections approximately two grade levels below the student's actual grade level. That means that *Sourcebook*, Grade 2, begins with what are normally considered pre-K selections. Then, by the end of each book, the last few selections are approximately on grade level.

How Are Selections Leveled?

The selections in each *Sourcebook* are leveled, starting with the easiest and progressing to the most difficult. The measure relied upon to order them in the *Sourcebooks* is Lexile levels. They are readability measurements that place readings on a common scale, beginning at 0 and going up to 1700. Reading programs, reading specialists, and the authors of this series all have used this readability measurement and found it useful. The Lexile Framework provides a standard way to assess the relative difficulty of selections.

How Does This Help?

Because the selections in each *Sourcebook* are leveled, you can start groups of students at the beginning, middle, or end of the book. Begin with selections that are easy for students to build their confidence. Then gradually work toward more challenging ones.

At the same time, use the additional books by the author and on the same theme that are suggested in this *Teacher's Guide.* Each *Sourcebook* lesson begins with recommendations of more books that are at or around the same Lexile level as the selection in the *Sourcebook*. The benefit of this plan is that it helps you locate a lot of books you can use. You can also keep track when students begin to read harder books, challenging and also supporting them.

The *Sourcebooks* will help you spend more time guiding students' learning than searching for the appropriate books. That part, at least, has already been done.

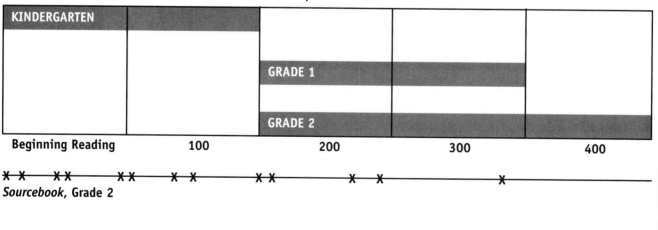

LEXILE / GRADE LEVEL

Sourcebook, Grade 2

HOW TO USE THIS BOOK

Guiding Struggling Learners

Frequently schools have classes with students of all ability levels, from a few grade levels below to one or two above grade level. Then, "average" students in one school district vary greatly from "average" students in a neighboring one. The *Sourcebook* series aims at those students who consistently rank in the lower 50 percent of text scores and national averages.

The *Sourcebook* offers a comprehensive program of student-appropriate literature, strategy-building, writing, revising, and reflecting. The approach is a holistic one. Rather than assigning a worksheet to attack a specific problem—say, comprehension—the *Sourcebook* addresses the broader problems as well.

Each *Sourcebook* weaves together a comprehensive network of skills (see pages 6–9) that brings together the appropriate literature, reading strategies for that literature, and prewriting, writing, and revising activities. Students who work through even two or three entire selections will benefit greatly by seeing the whole picture of reading actively and writing about the text. They will also benefit from the sense of accomplishment that comes through completion of a whole task and that results in creative, original work of their own—perhaps some of the first they have accomplished.

Working with Students in Groups

Students who are reading at the same level are often grouped together. Some students are often pulled out for special tutoring with trained reading tutors. Those students reading below grade level are placed in another group, those reading on level in still another group, and those reading above level in one or more other groups. For you as the teacher, the effort becomes how to juggle the various groups and keep them all on task.

That's where the *Sourcebook* comes in. Each lesson presents a sustained, meaningful assignment that can be targeted at specific groups in your class. Students show reluctance to read when the selection is too difficult or frustrating for them to read independently. With the *Sourcebook*, you can match the group to a selection at a Lexile level that is just right. Then you have a sustained, meaningful lesson to guide them through as well as a number of additional books for the group to read at the same level.

Integrating Lessons with Other Activities

Because *Sourcebook* lessons are comprehensive, you can integrate read-alouds, strategy lessons on comprehension, and word work on prefixes, suffixes, and base words. Each lesson affords you any number of opportunities to intervene at the right moment to guide students' learning.

Students can read selections silently to themselves and then work independently in one group while you are giving a strategy lesson with another group. Or, students may be reading independently any number of books on the same subject or theme.

Pulling Everything Together

The benefit of the *Sourcebook* comes in having everything pulled together in one place—for you and the student. You have 14 integrated units to choose from. Students have a book of their own, one they "own," that keeps them on track, guiding their learning and recording their progress. So, if you have interruptions because of holidays, field trips, or simply scheduling challenges, the *Sourcebook* holds the lesson together, allowing you and the students to double back if necessary and remember where they have been and where they are going.

Summary

While the *Sourcebook* will not fix every learning problem for every student, it will be helpful for struggling readers, especially those who are reading one or two grades below their academic grade. Reading and writing deficits are hard problems for students and require a great amount of effort—on the part of the teacher and the student—to make any real improvement. The *Sourcebook* is one useful tool in helping you create better readers and writers.

FREQUENTLY ASKED QUESTIONS

Because the *Sourcebooks* were extensively reviewed by teachers, a number of commonly asked questions have surfaced already, and the answers to them might be helpful in using the program.

1. Why is it called a *Sourcebook*?

The word *Sourcebook* captures a number of connotations and associations that seemed just right. For one, it is published by Great Source Education. The word *source* also had the right connotation of "place to go for a real, complete solution," as opposed to the other products that helped in only a limited area, such as "main idea" or "analogies." And, lastly, the term *Sourcebook* fit nicely alongside *Daybook,* another series also published by Great Source that targets better readers and writers who need help in critical reading, as opposed to this series that targets struggling readers.

2. Can students write in the *Sourcebook*?

Absolutely. Only by physically marking the text will students become truly active readers. To interact with a text and truly read as an active reader, students must write in the *Sourcebook*. The immediacy of reading and responding right there on the page is integral to the whole idea of the *Sourcebook*. By writing in the text, students build a sense of ownership about their work that is impossible to match through worksheets handed out week after week. The *Sourcebook* also serves, in a sense, like the student's portfolio and can become one of the most tangible ways of demonstrating a student's progress throughout the year.

3. Can I photocopy these lessons?

No, you cannot. Each page of the pupil's book carries a notice that explicitly states "copying is prohibited." To copy them illegally infringes on the rights of the authors of the selections and the publishers of the book. Writers such as Edward Marshall, Dorothy Carter, Byron Barton, and others have granted permission to use their work in the *Sourcebook*, but not the right to copy it.

You can, however, copy the blackline masters in this *Teacher's Guide*. These pages are intended for you to photocopy and use in the classroom and are marked clearly on each page.

4. Can I skip around in the *Sourcebook*?

Teachers will often want to skip around and adjust the *Sourcebook* to their curriculum. However, in *Sourcebooks* 2–5, the selections are, with few exceptions, sequenced in the order of the reading difficulty. Selections in Grade 2 progress from a Lexile reading level of 30 to 390. A similar progression exists at the other grade levels. The benefit comes in having selections you know will be appropriate for students and in having skills that are carefully sequenced. The writing expected of students progresses in difficulty just as the readability does, moving from easiest to hardest. Further, the word work skills build on one another, so that terms such as "plurals" and "suffixes" are assumed in later lessons after being introduced in earlier ones.

5. Where did the strategies used throughout the book come from?

Most of the reading strategies used are commonplace in elementary classrooms throughout the country. Reading textbooks as well as teacher resource books and in-services all describe the prereading and comprehension strategies used in the *Sourcebooks*. What is unusual in the *Sourcebooks* is the way these strategies have been woven together and applied to high-quality, appropriate literature.

6. Why do you direct students to read and reread the selection?

One suggestion from reviewers was to help struggling readers by asking them to do one thing at a time. Teachers suggested it was easier to read a selection once just to get a sense of it, a second time to respond to it in the Response Notes, and a third time to respond to the comprehension activities embedded in the selection. Rather than ask students to do three things at once, the lessons progress in manageable steps. It reduces frustration and increases chances of success. Plus, additional readings of a selection increase reading fluency and help increase comprehension.

7. Why do the *Sourcebooks* rely on Lexile measurements of readability?

The benefit of Lexile measurements are that they provide small increments of readability—say, from 220 to 240—and they are in wide use. The Lexile Framework for Reading has an easily accessed website (www.lexile.com) that allows you to search for authors and titles at specific readability levels. The website already has measured a huge selection of books and lexiled them. As a result, this measurement provides a public standard by which to assess readability and an ongoing tool for teachers.

8. How were the selections chosen and what is their readability?

Each selection in the *Sourcebooks* met numerous criteria: quality of the selection, readability, balance of fiction vs. nonfiction, as well as gender and ethnicity of the authors.

None of the criteria mattered if the selection did not hold the interest of students and didn't seem to be on a worthwhile subject or topic. But it is worth noting that 50 percent of the selections in the *Sourcebooks* are nonfiction, at the request of teachers who wanted more help with this genre.

9. How can I know if my students can read this literature?

You have a number of ways to know how well your students can read the selections. First, you can simply try out a lesson or two with students.

Second, you can also use a five- or ten-word vocabulary pretest as a quick indicator. Select five words randomly from each selection. Ask students to circle the ones they know and underline the ones they don't know. If students know only one to two words, then the selection will probably be frustrating for them. Spend some time preteaching the key vocabulary.

Third, ask students to read a selection aloud. By listening to the kind of miscues students make, you can gauge whether a selection is at, below, or above their reading level.

10. What if my students need even more help than what's in the *Sourcebook*?

This *Teacher's Guide* has been designed as the next level of support. Extra activities and blackline masters on vocabulary, comprehension, and assessment are included here so that they can be used at the teacher's discretion. These aids can help scaffold individual parts of lessons, giving more help with vocabulary, word work, or writing. But let students work through the lessons. Even if they make mistakes, they still may be making progress and may need only a little patience and encouragement. The *Sourcebooks* offer a good foundation for your curriculum.

ORGANIZATION

Book Organization

This **Sourcebook** has 14 selections organized sequentially from the easiest readability to the hardest. The first lesson begins with a selection at approximately two grade levels below the academic level. That is, **Sourcebook**, Grade 2, begins with two selections at Lexile 120 and Lexile 60, which is approximately early first grade and the middle of kindergarten.

Lesson Organization

Each lesson in the **Sourcebook** starts with an introduction that draws students into the selection, often by asking a provocative question or making a strong statement. The purpose of this introduction is to stimulate students' prior knowledge and build interest.

Opener

• Each selection begins with an introduction to create motivation for reading.

I. Before You Read

• Each lesson has three parts.

• The prereading step—the critical first step—builds background and further helps students access prior knowledge. Among the prereading strategies (see pages 41–44) included in **Part I** of this **Sourcebook** are:

• K-W-L
• Anticipation Guide
• Previewing
• Word Web

12

Duckling Days

By Karen Wallace

Look at the picture of the mother duck and her ducklings. How would you describe the ducklings? Write three or four words below to describe the ducklings.

125

I. **BEFORE YOU READ**

Predict and Preview

From the title *Duckling Days*, what do you think it will be about?

From the art on page 128, what do you think the reading will be about?

What do you think will happen in this reading?

MY PURPOSE

What are duckling days and what are they like?

126

II. Read

The reading step begins by telling students what they are to read and then details how students are to read the selection. The first step tells students how to mark the text. The second step reminds students to write their reactions or responses in "My Notes."
An example of an acceptable response is provided.

II. READ

Now read the story *Duckling Days* by Karen Wallace.
1. Read the story all the way through first.
2. Then come back and read the story again. This time write in "My Notes" how the story is like your life.
3. Then complete the "Stop and Retell" boxes.

My Notes

Example:

We live by a river, too.

Duckling Days
by Karen Wallace

In the grass beside the river a mother duck builds her nest.

She gathers grass and makes a hollow.

She lines her nest with downy feathers.

128

DUCKLING DAYS (continued)

In a nest beside the river a mother duck lays six white eggs.

She keeps them warm beneath her body.
Inside each egg a duckling grows.

My Notes

STOP and RETELL

What happens first in the story?

129

- Then, within each selection, a powerful comprehension strategy is embedded to help build in students the habits of good readers. Among the comprehension strategies included (see also pages 46–48) in Part II of this **Sourcebook** are:

- Stop and Think

- Stop and Explain

- Stop and Draw

- Stop and Retell

19

Then, at the end of each selection, students take time for Word Work to develop their word attack skills (see also pages 49–50.) Students who struggle to read in the early grades need help in breaking apart words to improve their reading fluency. The purpose of these activities is to help students know how to handle longer words. The first Word Work activity teaches elements of phonics. The second activity teaches elements of structure, including:

- prefixes and suffixes
- adding endings
- compound words
- syllables
- contractions
- plurals

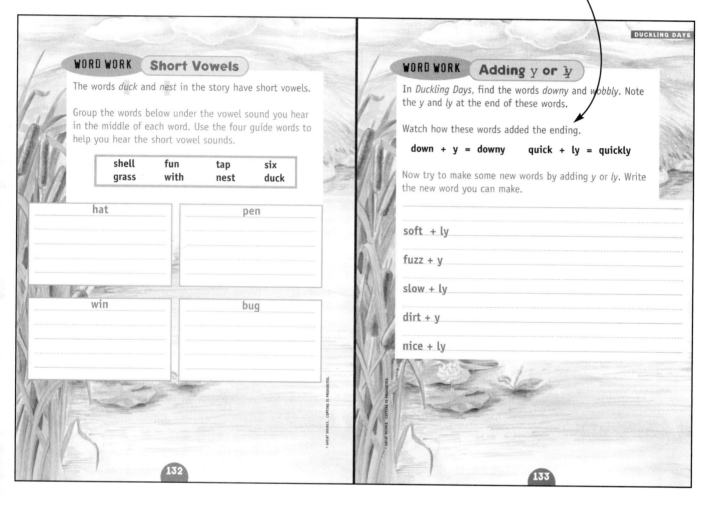

WORD WORK **Short Vowels**

The words *duck* and *nest* in the story have short vowels.

Group the words below under the vowel sound you hear in the middle of each word. Use the four guide words to help you hear the short vowel sounds.

shell	fun	tap	six
grass	with	nest	duck

hat

pen

win

bug

132

WORD WORK **Adding y or ly**

In *Duckling Days*, find the words *downy* and *wobbly*. Note the *y* and *ly* at the end of these words.

Watch how these words added the ending.

down + y = downy   quick + ly = quickly

Now try to make some new words by adding *y* or *ly*. Write the new word you can make.

soft + ly _____

fuzz + y _____

slow + ly _____

dirt + y _____

nice + ly _____

133

III. Write

The writing step begins with step-by-step instructions for building a writing assignment. Taken together, these instructions form the writing rubric for students to use in building the assignment. Here are some of the writing assignments for students:

- Sentence

- Narrative paragraph

- Journal entry

- Descriptive paragraph

- Poem

- Friendly letter

III. WRITE

Retell the story *Duckling Days*. Start by writing what happens in the beginning, middle, and end of the story.

Beginning
Write what happens on page 128 here.

Middle
Write what happens on page 129–130 here.

End
Write what happens on page 131 here.

134

TEACHER'S LESSON PLANS

Each lesson plan for the teacher of the *Sourcebook* has **12** pages:

PAGE 1 Background and Bibliography

- The lesson begins with background on the author and selection and gives at least three additional titles by this author or on this same subject.

- The additional titles in the bibliography are included both for read-alongs and as independent reading, giving you ways to introduce the author, selection, and general subject.

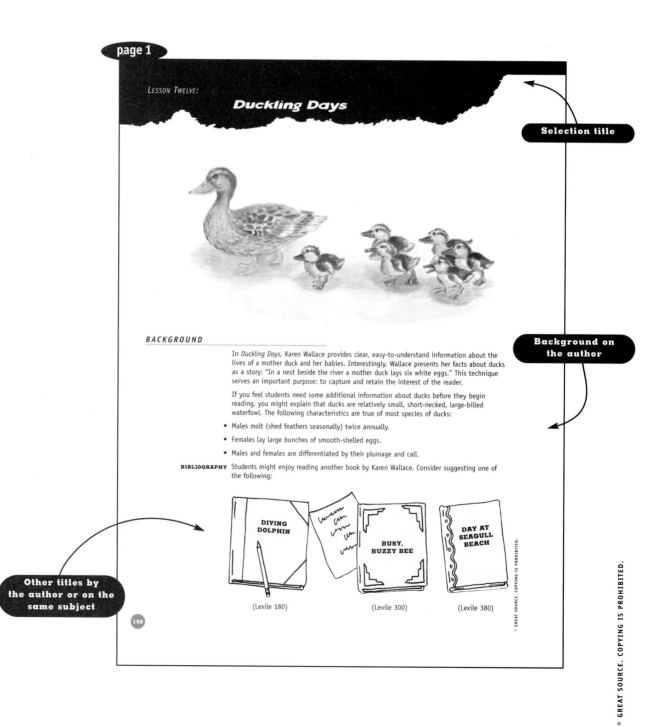

page 1

LESSON TWELVE:

Duckling Days

Selection title

BACKGROUND

In *Duckling Days*, Karen Wallace provides clear, easy-to-understand information about the lives of a mother duck and her babies. Interestingly, Wallace presents her facts about ducks as a story: "In a nest beside the river a mother duck lays six white eggs." This technique serves an important purpose: to capture and retain the interest of the reader.

If you feel students need some additional information about ducks before they begin reading, you might explain that ducks are relatively small, short-necked, large-billed waterfowl. The following characteristics are true of most species of ducks:

- Males molt (shed feathers seasonally) twice annually.
- Females lay large bunches of smooth-shelled eggs.
- Males and females are differentiated by their plumage and call.

BIBLIOGRAPHY Students might enjoy reading another book by Karen Wallace. Consider suggesting one of the following:

Background on the author

DIVING DOLPHIN

BUSY, BUZZY BEE

DAY AT SEAGULL BEACH

(Lexile 180)   (Lexile 300)   (Lexile 380)

Other titles by the author or on the same subject

190

PAGE 2 **How to Introduce the Reading**

- The next page of the teacher's plan introduces the selection and gives you a way to motivate students to read. In most cases, the introduction serves as a way to create a sense of expectation in students and to provide some initial background for the reading.

Other Reading

- Three more titles written at the same readability level are included in "Other Reading." The purpose is to suggest titles at this same reading level, so students can go beyond the selection in the text to other appropriate titles.

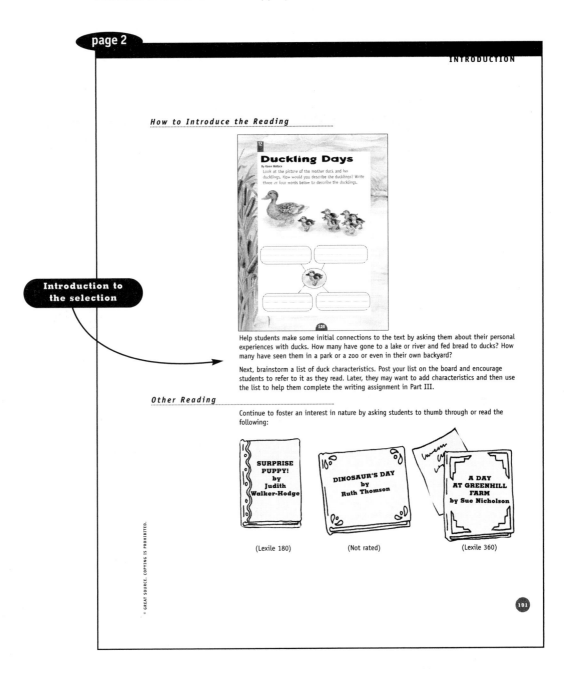

PAGE 3 Skills and Strategies Overview

Each lesson plan in the *Sourcebook* begins with a chart giving an overview of the skills covered in the lesson. The purpose is to give you an at-a-glance picture of the lesson.

Note in the chart the vocabulary words that are highlighted. These words from the selection are often presented in the **Vocabulary** blackline master to help familiarize students with key words in the selection.

Other Resources

Each lesson in the *Sourcebook* contains a wealth of additional resources to support you and your students. In all, <u>six blackline masters</u> provide additional scaffolding for you at critical parts of the lesson: Vocabulary, Prereading, Comprehension, Word Work (phonics), Word Work (structure), and Assessment.

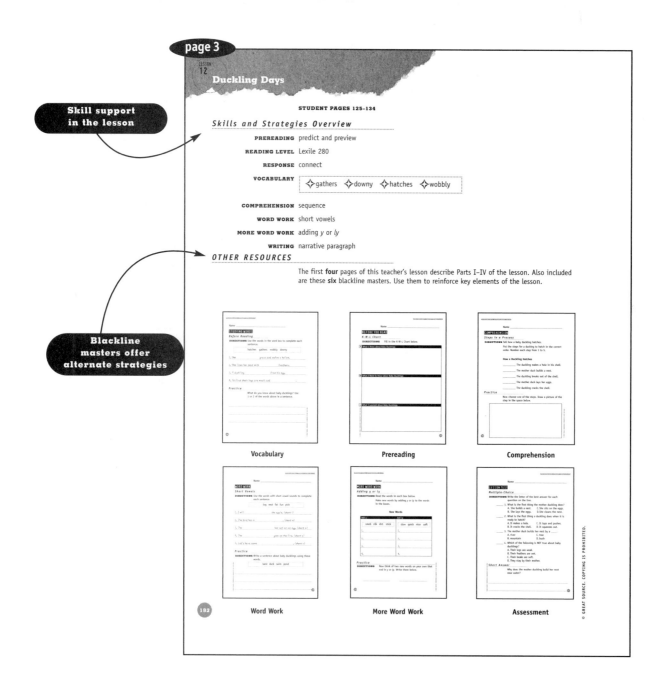

PAGE 4 Before You Read

- The *Teacher's Guide* walks through each lesson in the *Sourcebook,* following the three-step lesson plan and explaining how to teach each part.

- At each part, the appropriate blackline masters are cross-referenced.

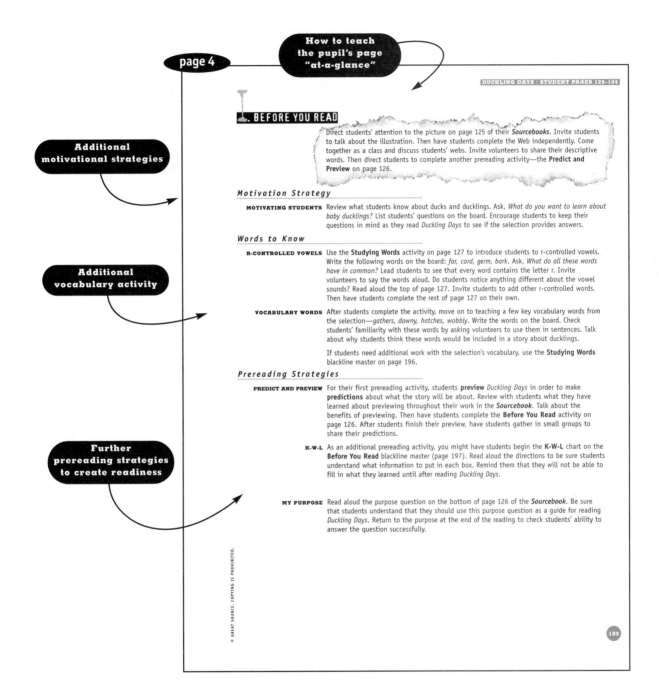

page 4

How to teach the pupil's page "at-a-glance"

DUCKLING DAYS / STUDENT PAGES 125–134

BEFORE YOU READ

Direct students' attention to the picture on page 125 of their *Sourcebooks*. Invite students to talk about the illustration. Then have students complete the Web independently. Come together as a class and discuss students' webs. Invite volunteers to share their descriptive words. Then direct students to complete another prereading activity—the **Predict and Preview** on page 126.

Additional motivational strategies

Motivation Strategy

MOTIVATING STUDENTS Review what students know about ducks and ducklings. Ask, *What do you want to learn about baby ducklings?* List students' questions on the board. Encourage students to keep their questions in mind as they read *Duckling Days* to see if the selection provides answers.

Words to Know

R-CONTROLLED VOWELS Use the **Studying Words** activity on page 127 to introduce students to r-controlled vowels. Write the following words on the board: *far, cord, germ, bark.* Ask, *What do all these words have in common?* Lead students to see that every word contains the letter r. Invite volunteers to say the words aloud. Do students notice anything different about the vowel sounds? Read aloud the top of page 127. Invite students to add other r-controlled words. Then have students complete the rest of page 127 on their own.

Additional vocabulary activity

VOCABULARY WORDS After students complete the activity, move on to teaching a few key vocabulary words from the selection—*gathers, downy, hatches, wobbly.* Write the words on the board. Check students' familiarity with these words by asking volunteers to use them in sentences. Talk about why students think these words would be included in a story about ducklings.

If students need additional work with the selection's vocabulary, use the **Studying Words** blackline master on page 196.

Prereading Strategies

PREDICT AND PREVIEW For their first prereading activity, students **preview** *Duckling Days* in order to make **predictions** about what the story will be about. Review with students what they have learned about previewing throughout their work in the *Sourcebook*. Talk about the benefits of previewing. Then have students complete the **Before You Read** activity on page 126. After students finish their preview, have students gather in small groups to share their predictions.

Further prereading strategies to create readiness

K-W-L As an additional prereading activity, you might have students begin the **K-W-L** chart on the **Before You Read** blackline master (page 197). Read aloud the directions to be sure students understand what information to put in each box. Remind them that they will not be able to fill in what they learned until after reading *Duckling Days*.

MY PURPOSE Read aloud the purpose question on the bottom of page 126 of the *Sourcebook*. Be sure that students understand that they should use this purpose question as a guide for reading *Duckling Days*. Return to the purpose at the end of the reading to check students' ability to answer the question successfully.

193

PAGE 5 **Read**

- In **Part II Read** students read the selection using an active reading strategy.

- Each **Part II Read** instructs students to read the selection once with an active reading strategy, and then read it again and write their thoughts or comments in "My Notes."

- **Reread** asks students to go back to the selection a third time to be sure they have answered all of the questions in the comprehension activity.

- **Word Work** gives suggestions for helping students with the phonics lesson in each selection.

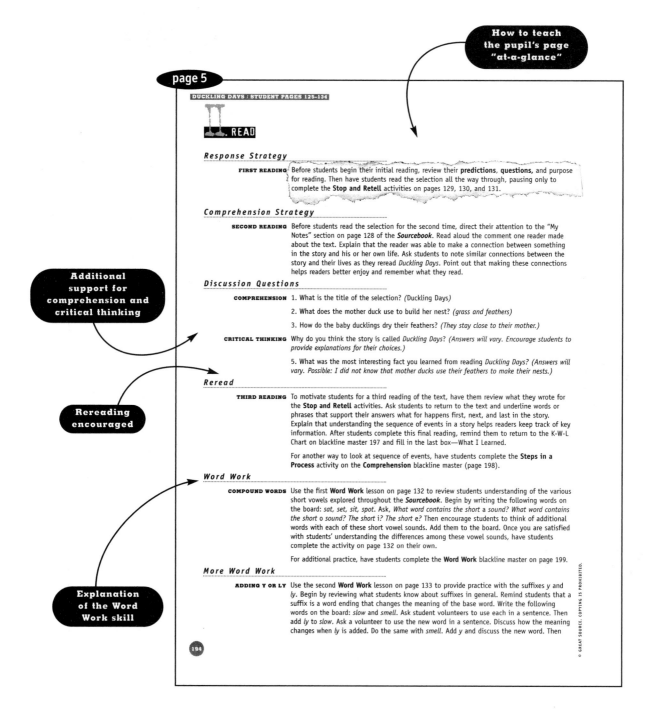

How to teach the pupil's page "at-a-glance"

page 5

DUCKLING DAYS / STUDENT PAGES 125–134

II. READ

Response Strategy

FIRST READING Before students begin their initial reading, review their **predictions**, **questions,** and purpose for reading. Then have students read the selection all the way through, pausing only to complete the **Stop and Retell** activities on pages 129, 130, and 131.

Comprehension Strategy

SECOND READING Before students read the selection for the second time, direct their attention to the "My Notes" section on page 128 of the *Sourcebook*. Read aloud the comment one reader made about the text. Explain that the reader was able to make a connection between something in the story and his or her own life. Ask students to note similar connections between the story and their lives as they reread *Duckling Days*. Point out that making these connections helps readers better enjoy and remember what they read.

Discussion Questions

COMPREHENSION 1. What is the title of the selection? *(Duckling Days)*

2. What does the mother duck use to build her nest? *(grass and feathers)*

3. How do the baby ducklings dry their feathers? *(They stay close to their mother.)*

CRITICAL THINKING Why do you think the story is called *Duckling Days*? *(Answers will vary. Encourage students to provide explanations for their choices.)*

5. What was the most interesting fact you learned from reading *Duckling Days*? *(Answers will vary. Possible: I did not know that mother ducks use their feathers to make their nests.)*

Reread

THIRD READING To motivate students for a third reading of the text, have them review what they wrote for the **Stop and Retell** activities. Ask students to return to the text and underline words or phrases that support their answers what for happens first, next, and last in the story. Explain that understanding the sequence of events in a story helps readers keep track of key information. After students complete this final reading, remind them to return to the K-W-L Chart on blackline master 197 and fill in the last box—What I Learned.

For another way to look at sequence of events, have students complete the **Steps in a Process** activity on the **Comprehension** blackline master (page 198).

Word Work

COMPOUND WORDS Use the first **Word Work** lesson on page 132 to review students understanding of the various short vowels explored throughout the *Sourcebook*. Begin by writing the following words on the board: *sat, set, sit, spot*. Ask, *What word contains the short a sound? What word contains the short o sound? The short i? The short e?* Then encourage students to think of additional words with each of these short vowel sounds. Add them to the board. Once you are satisfied with students' understanding of the differences among these vowel sounds, have students complete the activity on page 132 on their own.

For additional practice, have students complete the **Word Work** blackline master on page 199.

More Word Work

ADDING Y OR LY Use the second **Word Work** lesson on page 133 to provide practice with the suffixes *y* and *ly*. Begin by reviewing what students know about suffixes in general. Remind students that a suffix is a word ending that changes the meaning of the base word. Write the following words on the board: *slow* and *smell*. Ask student volunteers to use each in a sentence. Then add *ly* to *slow*. Ask a volunteer to use the new word in a sentence. Discuss how the meaning changes when *ly* is added. Do the same with *smell*. Add *y* and discuss the new word. Then

194

© GREAT SOURCE. COPYING IS PROHIBITED.

Additional support for comprehension and critical thinking

Rereading encouraged

Explanation of the Word Work skill

PAGE 6 **More Word Work, Write, and Look Back**

- The page begins with additional help with the second **Word Work** lesson. This lesson deals with structure issues, such as plurals, suffixes, and compound words.

- Next, the students write. Explicit instructions on the assignment are included in the pupil's text.

- The Writing Rubric gives teachers a way to evaluate students' writing.

- The lesson ends by encouraging students to look back and reflect on what they have read and references a Readers' Checklist. The Assessment blackline master is also cross-referenced here.

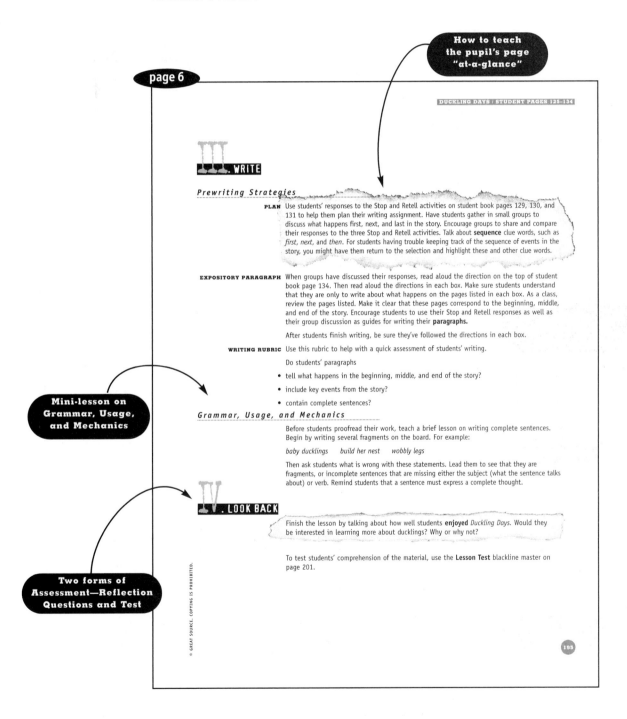

How to teach the pupil's page "at-a-glance"

page 6

DUCKLING DAYS / STUDENT PAGES 129–134

WRITE

Prewriting Strategies

PLAN Use students' responses to the Stop and Retell activities on student book pages 129, 130, and 131 to help them plan their writing assignment. Have students gather in small groups to discuss what happens first, next, and last in the story. Encourage groups to share and compare their responses to the three Stop and Retell activities. Talk about **sequence** clue words, such as *first*, *next*, and *then*. For students having trouble keeping track of the sequence of events in the story, you might have them return to the selection and highlight these and other clue words.

EXPOSITORY PARAGRAPH When groups have discussed their responses, read aloud the direction on the top of student book page 134. Then read aloud the directions in each box. Make sure students understand that they are only to write about what happens on the pages listed in each box. As a class, review the pages listed. Make it clear that these pages correspond to the beginning, middle, and end of the story. Encourage students to use their Stop and Retell responses as well as their group discussion as guides for writing their **paragraphs.**

After students finish writing, be sure they've followed the directions in each box.

WRITING RUBRIC Use this rubric to help with a quick assessment of students' writing.

Do students' paragraphs

- tell what happens in the beginning, middle, and end of the story?

- include key events from the story?

- contain complete sentences?

Grammar, Usage, and Mechanics

Before students proofread their work, teach a brief lesson on writing complete sentences. Begin by writing several fragments on the board. For example:

baby ducklings   build her nest   wobbly legs

Then ask students what is wrong with these statements. Lead them to see that they are fragments, or incomplete sentences that are missing either the subject (what the sentence talks about) or verb. Remind students that a sentence must express a complete thought.

LOOK BACK

Finish the lesson by talking about how well students **enjoyed** *Duckling Days*. Would they be interested in learning more about ducklings? Why or why not?

To test students' comprehension of the material, use the **Lesson Test** blackline master on page 201.

Mini-lesson on Grammar, Usage, and Mechanics

Two forms of Assessment—Reflection Questions and Test

© GREAT SOURCE. COPYING IS PROHIBITED.

195

Each lesson plan in the *Sourcebook Teacher's Guide* has six blackline masters for additional levels of support for key skill areas.

PAGE 7 Studying Words

- Each **Studying Words** blackline master helps students learn the meanings of a few words from the selection. The purpose of this blackline master is to expose students to the meanings of four to five key words in the selection, giving them readiness before they read.

Meanings of words from the selection are taught.

page 7

Name _____

STUDYING WORDS

Before Reading

DIRECTIONS Use the words in the word box to complete each sentence.

| hatches   gathers   wobbly   downy |

1. She _____ grass and makes a hollow.

2. She lines her nest with _____ feathers.

3. A duckling _____ from his egg.

4. At first their legs are weak and _____ .

Practice

What do you know about baby ducklings? Use 1 or 2 of the words above in a sentence.

_____

_____

_____

_____

Vocabulary pre-teaches important words from the selection.

196

PAGE 8 Before You Read

- An additional prereading activity is included to ensure that students have sufficient background for reading the selection. Generally the purpose of the activities is to activate students' prior knowledge about a subject and help them predict what the selection is about.

page 8

Additional prereading activity builds background and activates students' prior knowledge.

Name _____

BEFORE YOU READ

K-W-L Chart

DIRECTIONS   Fill in the K-W-L Chart below.

K What I Know about Baby Ducklings

W What I Want to Know about Baby Ducklings

L What I Learned about Baby Ducklings

197

PAGE 9 Comprehension

- Each **Comprehension** blackline master affords teachers still another way to build students' understanding of the selection, using a different strategy from the one found in the *Sourcebook*.

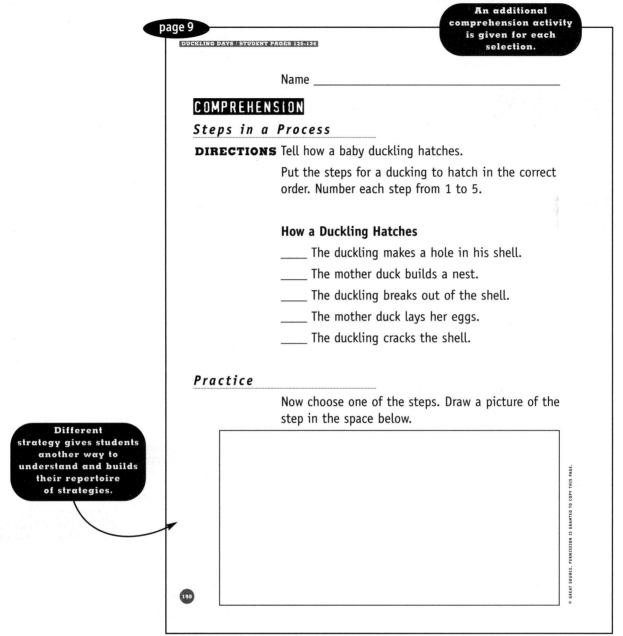

page 9

An additional comprehension activity is given for each selection.

DUCKLING DAYS / STUDENT PAGES 125–134

Name _____

COMPREHENSION

Steps in a Process

DIRECTIONS Tell how a baby duckling hatches.

Put the steps for a ducking to hatch in the correct order. Number each step from 1 to 5.

How a Duckling Hatches

____ The duckling makes a hole in his shell.

____ The mother duck builds a nest.

____ The duckling breaks out of the shell.

____ The mother duck lays her eggs.

____ The duckling cracks the shell.

Practice

Now choose one of the steps. Draw a picture of the step in the space below.

Different strategy gives students another way to understand and builds their repertoire of strategies.

198

© GREAT SOURCE. PERMISSION IS GRANTED TO COPY THIS PAGE.

PAGES 10 AND 11 Word Work

- Each **Word Work** activity offers additional practice on the phonics skill shown in the pupil's book. Often students will need repeated practice on a skill before they internalize it.

- **More Word Work** blackline masters give students practice in the word structure skill from the pupil's book.

page 10

Extra practice on phonics skill

Pages build on words from selection

Name _____

WORD WORK

Short Vowels

DIRECTIONS Use the words with short vowel sounds to complete each sentence.

log nest fat fun pick

1. *I will* _____ *the apple.* (short i)

2. *The bird has a* _____ . (short e)

3. *The* _____ *hen sat on an egg.* (short a)

4. *The* _____ *goes on the fire.* (short o)

5. *Let's have some* _____ . (short u)

Practice

DIRECTIONS Write a sentence about baby ducklings using these words.

land duck swim pond

page 11

Extra practice on word structure skill

Name _____

MORE WORD WORK

Adding y or ly

DIRECTIONS Read the words in each box below.
Make new words by adding *y* or *ly* to the words in the boxes.

New Words

Add y	Add ly
smell silk dirt stick	slow quick nice soft
1.	1.
2.	2.
3.	3.
4.	4.

Practice

DIRECTIONS Now think of two new words on your own that end in *y* or *ly*. Write them below.

Repeated practice helps students remember the skill.

PAGE 12 Lesson Test

- Each lesson in the *Sourcebook* ends with the opportunity for students to reflect on their reading. This self-assessment is an informal inventory of what they learned from the reading.

- The **Lesson Test** blackline master gives a multiple-choice test on the selection.

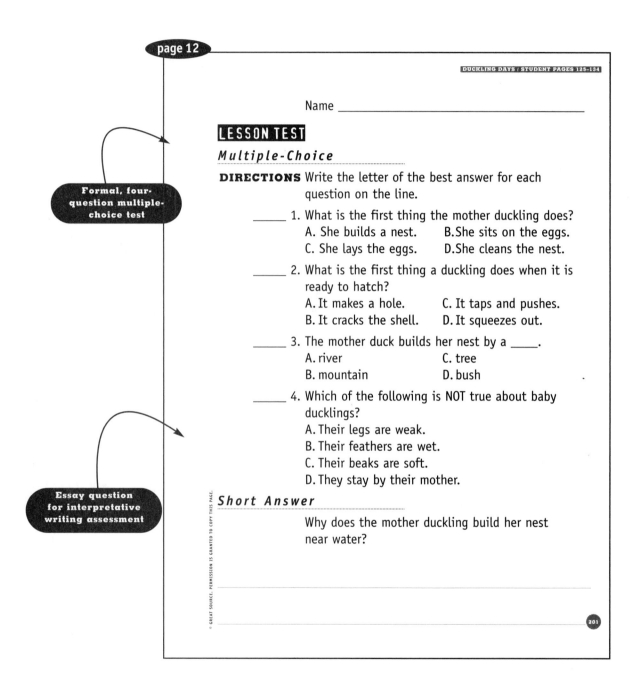

page 12

DUCKLING DAYS / STUDENT PAGES 129–134

Name _____

LESSON TEST

Multiple-Choice

DIRECTIONS Write the letter of the best answer for each question on the line.

_____ 1. What is the first thing the mother duckling does?
   A. She builds a nest.   B. She sits on the eggs.
   C. She lays the eggs.   D. She cleans the nest.

_____ 2. What is the first thing a duckling does when it is ready to hatch?
   A. It makes a hole.   C. It taps and pushes.
   B. It cracks the shell.   D. It squeezes out.

_____ 3. The mother duck builds her nest by a _____.
   A. river   C. tree
   B. mountain   D. bush

_____ 4. Which of the following is NOT true about baby ducklings?
   A. Their legs are weak.
   B. Their feathers are wet.
   C. Their beaks are soft.
   D. They stay by their mother.

Short Answer

Why does the mother duckling build her nest near water?

_____

_____

201

Formal, four-question multiple-choice test

Essay question for interpretative writing assessment

Guiding Students' Reading

BY LAURA ROBB

Whenever I coach teachers, I meet with them to learn about their teaching styles and practices and their educational philosophy, and all the time I'm jotting down questions they have for me. At a school in my community, I recently met with teachers from grades 2, 3, 4, and 5. Their teaching experience ranged from two to ten years, and their teaching styles included a reading/writing workshop that integrated the language arts and a more structured classroom that separated topics such as reading, writing, spelling, grammar, and punctuation skills. However, among 12 teachers, three questions surfaced again and again:

1. What can I do to support *all my readers,* including those who struggle?

2. How do I find short materials for my struggling and reluctant readers?

3. Can I apply the guided reading principles primary teachers are using to older students?

Reflective teachers constantly pose questions, for questions are the foundation of inquiry. And inquiry can lead to responsive teaching—teaching that meets the needs of each child in your classroom as well as spurs teachers to explore answers to their questions.

In this article, I will address the three questions because they are crucial to supporting teachers who understand the importance of taking each struggling or reluctant reader where he or she is and gently nudging him or her forward by offering chunks of independent reading time, scaffolding instruction, and organizing and leading flexible strategic reading groups.

Independent Reading

Too often, struggling readers spend more of their time completing skill sheets than reading books they can enjoy. The skill-sheet instructional strategy comes from the traditional belief that isolated practice of such skills as finding the main idea, sequencing, learning word meanings, and syllabication would help students acquire the skills to read books, the newspapers, and magazines.

Contrary to tradition, research shows that one of teachers' most important tasks regarding comprehension instruction is to set aside ample time for actual text reading. Students who struggle need to read as much as or more than proficient readers—providing the texts are at their independent reading level. Such daily silent reading combined with strategy demonstrations and student practice can improve reading more than a diet of skill sheets.

Finding adequate materials for struggling readers who read one or more years below grade level is a challenge. Teachers recognize that there is a limited amount of easy-to-read material available for middle-grade students—reading materials that are on topics that hold their interest from start to finish.

The *Sourcebooks*, however, are outstanding resources for teachers in need of independent reading materials. Selections are leveled from easy reading at the start of each student book to a final lesson that's near or on grade level. Since selections are excerpts from the finest literature, teachers have 12 to 16 books per grade level that children can read independently throughout the school year. Moreover, teachers can offer other readable books by the authors students enjoy most. For those who require teacher support while reading, you can scaffold instruction by sitting beside a student and guide the reading with questions, prompts, and modeling.

The Importance of Scaffolding

Scaffolding is the specific support offered to pairs, small groups, individuals, and the entire class that teachers provide before, during, and after reading. Teachers scaffold students' reading until each student demonstrates an understanding of a strategy. Gradually, the teacher withdraws support, moving students to independence.

In a typical middle-grade classroom, where teachers work with a mix of reluctant/struggling, grade level, and proficient readers, scaffolding reading might start with the entire class, then move to those students who require additional help in order to understand and internalize a strategy.

Recent research shows that applying reading strategies to texts—strategies such as predicting, questioning, and making personal connections—improves students' comprehension before, during, and after reading. In addition, it's important to help students set purposes for reading before plunging them into a text, for this strategy focuses students on what's important in the selection.

Good teaching provides scaffolding for proficient and struggling readers and starts before reading, helping students activate their prior knowledge and experience so they can use what they know to connect to the authors' words and construct new understandings. During reading, scaffolding strategies build on setting purposes for reading as students actively interact with a text by using the reading purposes to underline words and phrases and write notes in the margin. After reading, scaffolding improves recall and deepens comprehension as students practice such strategies as rereading and skimming to answer a question, to find details about a character or an event, to locate information, or to prepare for writing. Reflecting on their reading by revisiting the piece, talking to a partner, and writing about what they've read all boost comprehension and recall of key details and ideas.

Why Sourcebooks Are a Must-Have Text

We have carefully structured each *Sourcebook* lesson so that it builds on the sound, current research on scaffolding instruction and the reading strategy curriculum. We've integrated the strategic parts of each lesson to heighten the impact on struggling readers of practicing and coming to understand related strategies. Here's the support your students will receive with each lesson:

Get Ready to Read: throughout the *Sourcebook*, students practice four to six research-tested activities that prepare them for reading.

Your Purpose for Reading: each lesson sets a purpose for reading that builds on the preparation activity and focuses students' reading goals.

Read and Interact with the Text: during the first reading, students become **active readers**, underlining and circling parts of the text, then writing their thoughts and questions in the Notes.

Comprehension Builders: while reading, students are invited to stop and think about the story's structure and meaning, as well as answer questions and think about relationships such as cause and effect.

Word Work: these activities help struggling readers improve their decoding strategies and learn how they can build on what they already know about words to figure out how to say new, unfamiliar words.

Build Vocabulary: extra word work pages in each unit deepen children's knowledge of letter/sound relationships and expand their vocabulary.

Develop Strategic Reading Strength: students practice applying to the selections reading strategies such as predict/support, visualize, make connections, and retell and explain. Practice fosters students' ability to use strategies to make meaning while reading all kinds of texts.

Writing Activity: always related to the reading selection, students use their plans to write letters, poems, and expository, descriptive, and narrative paragraphs.

© GREAT SOURCE. COPYING IS PROHIBITED.

Many of your students will be able to work through each lesson independently or with the support of a reading partner. However, there will be times when you will use the entire lesson or parts of a lesson with a pair or small group of students. Moreover, you'll find the *Sourcebook* lessons are ideal for group instruction because short, readable selections allow you to focus on strategies and work through part of a lesson in one to two periods.

Strategic Reading Groups

"I can't read this stuff. I'll never learn how to read." These comments, made by readers who struggle, reveal how fragile these youngsters are. Unfortunately, their self-esteem is low due to all their negative experiences with reading. At school, they watch classmates complete work easily and achieve success—these observations only reinforce struggling learners' negative thoughts about their ability to progress. At home, they avoid reading because they can't cope with grade-level texts. Often, teachers and parents read materials to them. However, this only improves students' listening. To improve reading, students must read books they CAN read and enjoy.

The best way to support your struggling readers is to organize groups that are flexible, because they respond to the ever-changing needs of students.

Responsive Grouping

Learners improve at different rates. That's why responsive grouping, where you work with students who have common needs, is the key to moving all readers forward. Once a student understands how to apply a strategy such as predicting, posing questions, or previewing, it's time to move that child to a group that's working on another strategy.

Responsive, flexible grouping is similar to the guided reading model primary teachers use. The emphasis of instruction is on developing critical thinking strategies, interpreting the meaning of texts, and learning to find the main points an author is making. In addition, those students who need to bolster their ability to pronounce long, new words and figure out their meanings using context clues receive ongoing teacher support. The question, then, that faces all of us teachers is, "How do I monitor the progress of each child so I can respond to his/her reading needs by changing group membership?"

First, teachers must systematically observe their students by doing the following:

- Jot down notes as students work independently, with a partner, or in a small group.

- Study samples of students' written work.

- Observe students during teacher-led small-group strategic reading lessons.

- Hold short one-on-one conferences and listen to students answer questions about their reading process, progress, and needs.

- Use this data to adjust group membership.

The following chart compares Responsive and Traditional Grouping. It will help you understand the benefits of responsive grouping.

Responsive Grouping	Traditional Grouping
Students grouped by assessment of a specific strategy.	Students grouped by general assessments such as standardized testing.
Responds to students' needs and changes as these needs change.	Static and unchanging for long periods of time.
Strategies practiced before, during, and after reading with a variety of genres.	Selections limited to basal. Worksheets for specific skills.
Books chosen for the group at their instructional level.	Students move through a grade-level basal whether or not they read above or below grade level.
Reading is in silent, meaningful chunks.	Round-robin oral reading.
Students actively interact with the text, discuss and reflect on it, and develop critical thinking.	Students read to find out the correct answer.
Varied vocabulary with an emphasis on solving word problems while reading.	Controlled vocabulary.
Students practice and apply strategies that enable them to connect to and think deeply about their reading.	Students complete worksheets that have little to do with the story in the basal anthology.
Students learn to apply word-solving strategies to real books.	Students practice skills with worksheets. The transfer to using word-solving strategies in real books is rarely made.
Evaluation based on careful observation of students' reading in a variety of situations.	Evaluation based on skill sheets and basal reading texts.

The Sourcebooks and Responsive Grouping

The **Sourcebooks** are ideal for small-group work that focuses on a specific reading or writing strategy. Selections are readable, and all the strategies are connected and/or related in each lesson. Moreover, you don't have to use valuable time to search for short materials to frame a meaningful lesson that can nudge struggling readers forward.

If one child or a group of children is/are experiencing difficulty with a specific strategy such as previewing, taking notes, decoding, or preparing to write, the **Sourcebooks** are the perfect resource for the teacher to support and guide those students. Teachers can focus on one part of a lesson with the group or work through an entire lesson over several days. The main consideration is to offer instructional scaffolding to readers who struggle, for as you work together, you will improve their reading ability and develop their confidence and self-esteem.

Ten Suggestions for Supporting Struggling Readers

The tips that follow are from a list that I keep in my lesson plan book, so I can revisit it and make sure I am attending to the needs of every student who requires my support.

1. **Be positive.** Focus your energies on what students can do. Accept students where they are and use the *Sourcebook* lessons to move them forward.

2. **Set reasonable and doable goals with your students.** Continue to revise the goals as students improve.

3. **Give students reading materials they can read independently**, such as the selections in the *Sourcebook*. When students DO the reading, they will improve. Help students select reading materials at their comfort level and encourage them to read, read, read! The research of Richard Allington shows that when students continually read many texts that are enjoyable and at their comfort level, they make progress.

4. **Get students actively involved** with their learning by using strategies that ask students to interact instead of to passively listen.

5. **Help students learn a strategy or information a different way** if the method you've introduced isn't working.

6. **Sit side-by-side and explain** a point or strategy to a student who needs extra scaffolding. Closing the gap between your explanation and the student can result in improved comprehension.

7. **Invite students to retell information** to a partner or in small groups. Talk helps learners remember and clarify their ideas.

8. **Make sure students understand directions.**

9. **Help struggling readers see their progress.** Invite students to reflect on their progress and tell you about it. Or tell students the progress you see.

10. **Give students extra time** to complete work and tests.

Closing Thoughts

Using the *Sourcebooks* with your reluctant and struggling readers can transform passive, unengaged readers into active and motivated learners. As your students complete the *Sourcebook* lessons and benefit from other parts of your reading curriculum, they will have had many opportunities to build their self-confidence and self-esteem and to develop a repertoire of helpful strategies by participating in reading, writing, and thinking experiences that are positive and continue to move them forward.

Allington, Richard. *What Really Matters for Struggling Readers: Designing Research-Based Programs.* New York: Longman, 2001.

Fountas, Irene, and Gay Su Pinnell. *Guided Reading: Good First Teaching for All Children*. Portsmouth, NH: Heinemann, 1996.

Gillet, Jean Wallace, and Charles Temple. *Understanding Reading Problems: Assessment and Instruction,* 3rd ed. New York: HarperCollins, 1990.

Robb, Laura. *Teaching Reading in Middle School*. New York: Scholastic, 2000.

BY RUTH NATHAN

During the past 30 years, many studies centering on the reading process have identified what good readers do (NRP, 2000; Pressley and Woloshyn, 1995). We know they use efficient strategies to comprehend and that they know when and where to use them. We know, too, that good readers monitor their comprehension, and that they are appropriately reflective. That is, strong readers know when they need to read more, read again, or ask for help. Proficient readers also possess strong vocabularies and usually have vast backgrounds of experience, either real or vicarious.

In order to grow into becoming a proficient reader, studies from the fields of both psychology and education have also shown that successful instruction will most likely occur when certain needs are met (Adams, 1990). For example, it is important for readers to be reading at their instructional level when they're learning comprehension strategies and not be frustrated by text that is too difficult. Difficult text usually has more complex syntactic structures and less-frequent words. It is equally important that teachers teach a few (one or two) strategies at a time, in context, and that these strategies be repeated frequently.

Because of what we know about proficient readers *and* quality instruction, the chapters in this *Sourcebook* have embraced three keys to promote student success:

KEY ONE: Only a few comprehension strategies are taught at a time, and these comprehension strategies are taught *in* context, practiced, and repeated (Harvey and Goudvis, 2000; Kamil, Mosenthal, Pearson, and Barr, 2000; Robb, 2000).

KEY TWO: The literature in the *Sourcebook* is of high interest and appropriate readability. This means that the stories selected will interest readers at this age; that the syntactic complexity is low at first, becoming ever-more difficult; and that word recognition is eased by choosing books with more frequent words and fewer rare words. Only gradually do stories contain a greater number of rare words.

KEY THREE: In each chapter, rare words are identified and explained. In addition, there are word recognition exercises in each chapter meant to help less-proficient readers gain in their word-recognition power. Students review sound/symbol correspondences and learn new correspondences, as well. Additionally, they are shown how to use analogy to read new words as well as how to use word parts, such as syllables and suffixes, to speed word recognition.

In addition to the three keys, the authors of the *Sourcebook* have utilized many strategies *before*, *during*, and *after* reading to engage readers and to promote transfer of learning.

Each chapter begins with readers accessing their prior knowledge and suggests a reason for reading. Research has shown prior knowledge and purpose to be important factors in comprehension (Adams, 1990). During reading, students are encouraged to talk with classmates, thus articulating their beliefs while at the same time hearing other interpretations of the text (Booth and Barton, 2000; Keene and Zimmermann, 1997). In addition, during reading students are using the text pages to reflect on their understanding through invitations to both write and draw (Clagget, 1999; Harvey and Goudvis, 2000). This practice goes back to the Middle Ages, but has received much support in all contemporary models of competent thinking (Pressley and Woloshyn, 1995). After reading, students are using all the language arts—reading, writing, listening, and speaking, as well as drawing—to write related entries, be it a summary, an invitation, a journal entry with a point of view, or a creative story ending or poem.

All in all, the *Sourcebooks* are the perfect answer to what struggling readers need to improve their comprehension and reading enjoyment. The three keys to success combined with before-, during-, and after-reading opportunities will provide students with many meaningful and joyful experiences. Our hope is that these experiences might lead students to a life filled with unforgettable encounters with texts of all types—books, newspapers, magazines, and all texts electronic.

Four Must-Have Teacher Resources

Classrooms That Work: They Can All Read and Write, 2nd ed., by Patricia M. Cunningham and Richard L. Allington. New York: Longman, 1999.

This book covers a range of topics: teaching reading and writing in the primary and intermediate grades. You'll visit classrooms that use Cunningham's "Four Blocks" approach to reading and better understand how the model works in the primary grades.

Easy Mini-Lessons for Building Vocabulary by Laura Robb. New York: Scholastic, 1999.

Choose from a large menu of doable strategies that build students' vocabulary before, during, and after reading. You'll also help prepare your students for standardized tests with the "Test-Taking Tips" sprinkled throughout the book.

Words Their Way: Word Study for Phonics, Vocabulary, and Spelling Instruction, 2nd ed., by Donald R. Bear, Marcia Invernizzi, Francine Johnston, and Shane Templeton. Columbus, OH: Merrill, 2000.

This book will strengthen teachers' knowledge of word study and spelling by clearly explaining developmental spelling and each of the stages children pass through. In addition, the book is packed with easy-to-implement word study games and lessons that can improve children's ability to read and understand multi-syllable words.

Reading with *Meaning: Teaching Comprehension* in the *Primary Grades*, by Debbie Miller, Portland, ME: Stenhouse, 2002.

In this thought-provoking book, teachers will read about techniques for modeling thinking; specific examples of modeled strategy lessons for inferring, asking questions, making connections, determining importance in text, creating mental images, and synthesizing information.

Other References

Adams, Marilyn Jager. *Beginning to Read: Thinking and Learning about Print.* Cambridge, MA: Bradford, 1990.

Harvey, Stephanie and Anne Goudvis. *Strategies That Work: Teaching Comprehension to Enhance Understanding.* Portland, ME: Stenhouse, 2000.

Kamil, Michael L., Peter B. Mosenthal, P. David Person, and Rebecca Barr. *Handbook of Reading Research: Volume III.* Mahwah, NJ: Lawrence Erlbaum Associates, 2000.

Keene, Ellin Oliver and Susan Zimmerman. *Mosaic of Thought: Teaching Comprehension in a Reader's Workshop.* Portsmouth, NH: Heinemann, 1997.

National Reading Panel. *National Reading Panel: Teaching Children to Read: Reports of the Subgroups.* Washington, DC: National Institute of Child Health and Human Development/Department of Education, 2000.

Norton, Donna E. *Through the Eyes of a Child: An Introduction to Children's Literature*, 6th ed. Upper Saddle River, NJ: Merrill/Prentice Hall, 2003.

Pressley, Michael and Vera Woloshyn. *Cognitive Strategy Instruction that Really Improves Children's Academic Performance*, 2nd ed. Cambridge, MA: Brookline, 1995.

Robb, Laura. *Teaching Reading in the Middle School: A Strategic Approach to Teaching Reading that Improves Comprehension and Thinking.* New York: Scholastic, 2000.

Here is a quick guide to the main prereading, comprehension, and reflective strategies used in the *Sourcebooks*. Students will benefit from explicit instruction in these strategies. You can help teach these strategies by introducing them to students and then modeling how to use them.

In order to help students absorb and internalize the strategies and overview, we've repeated them in different lessons so that students could encounter them many times throughout the book.

Overview

Prereading Strategies

K-W-L

Anticipation Guide

Preview

Word Web

Active Reading Strategies

Make Clear

Connect

Question

Draw

Comprehension Strategies

Stop and Think/Stop and Explain

Stop and Draw

Stop and Retell

Word Work Skills

Word Work Activities

Rhyme Book

Silly Sentences

Odd One Out

Word Sort

PREREADING STRATEGIES

K - W - L

What It Is

K-W-L is a pre- and post-reading strategy designed to facilitate students' interest in and activate their prior knowledge of a topic before reading nonfiction material. The letters *K, W,* and *L* stand for "What I Know," "What I Want to Know," and "What I Learned."

Look at the example of a K-W-L chart from Grade 2, Lesson 3, *Bread, Bread, Bread:*

KNOW

Rolls are bread.

WANT

What are other kinds of bread?

LEARN

People everywhere eat bread.

How to Introduce It

Introduce K-W-L as a whole-class activity. Give students time to write one or two questions they have. Explain that they will come back to their chart after they have finished reading, to record what they have learned.

Explain to students that K-W-L first pulls together what they know and then gives them questions that supply a purpose for reading.

Be sure to return to the chart and have students list what they learned in the *L* column.

Why It Works

Brainstorming (the *K* part) activates prior knowledge. What sets K-W-L apart from other prereading strategies is that K-W-L also encourages students to ask questions (the *W* component), thereby setting meaningful purposes for their reading. Returning to the chart (the *L* component) brings closure to the activity and demonstrates the purposefulness of the task.

Comments and Cautions

Don't worry about the accuracy of what students write under the *K* column. Students can correct any errors later during the *L* part of the activity.

After students write what they know, under *K*, ask them to get together in groups. This will help readers benefit from the knowledge of the group collectively.

Then, as students break out of their groups to begin reading, be sure to focus them on their questions under *W*, "What I Want to Know."

Anticipation Guide

What It Is

An anticipation guide is a series of statements that students respond to, first individually and then as a group, before reading a selection. The intent is not to quiz students but to prompt answers and the discussion that ensues. The discussion will build background and expectation and give students a motivating reason to read.

Here is an example from **Sourcebook,** Grade 2, Lesson 4, "Sam's Story":

Which animals get along with each other? Which ones don't?

Read each sentence and circle whether it is true or false.
Share your ideas with a partner.

True	False	**Dogs like to chase cats.**
True	False	**Cats like to chase mice.**
True	False	**Cats will chase birds.**
True	False	**Birds and dogs always get along together.**
True	False	**All animals are friends.**

How to Introduce It

Have students read the statements. (When making your own guides, keep the number of statements to about four to five items. More than that makes it difficult to discuss in detail.)

Discuss the students' responses. The point of an anticipation guide is to discuss students' various answers and explore their opinions. Discussion builds the prior knowledge of each student by adding to it the prior knowledge of other students. The discussion of anticipation guide statements can also be a powerful motivator because once students have answered them, they have a stake in seeing if they are "right."

Encourage students to make predictions about what the selection will be about based on the statements.

Then read the selection.

After reading the selection, have students return to their guides and reevaluate their responses based on what they learned from the selection.

Why It Works

Anticipation guides are useful tools for eliciting predictions before reading, both with fiction and nonfiction. By encouraging students to think critically about a series of statements, anticipation guides raise expectations and build excitement about the selection.

Comments and Cautions

This is a highly motivational prereading activity. Try to keep the class discussion on the subject; the teacher's role is that of a facilitator, encouraging students to examine and re-examine their responses. The greater the stake students have in an opinion, the more they will be motivated to read about the issue.

The focus of the guide should not be on whether students' responses are "correct," but rather on the discussion that ensues once students complete the guide individually.

You might also turn the entire anticipation guide process into a whole-group activity by having students respond with either "thumbs up" or "thumbs down."

Preview

What It Is

Previewing is a prereading strategy in which students read the title and skim the selection and then reflect on a few key questions. It asks the students to "sample" the selection before they begin reading and functions very much like the preview to a movie.

Look at the example from Grade 2, Lesson 1, *I Am an Apple*:

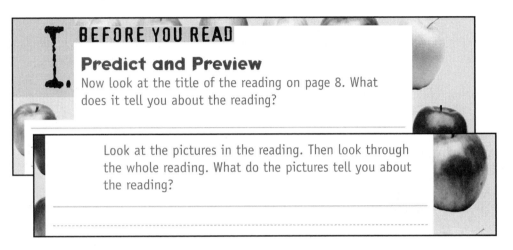

How to Introduce It

Previewing can be done as an individual or group activity. You might introduce it to the group and in later lessons encourage students to work on their own.

The first time you use this activity, take time to model previewing carefully for students.

Direct them to the title. Have a student read it aloud.

Then ask them to look at the first sentence. Have someone read it aloud.

Give students 10–15 seconds to look over the rest of the selection. Ask them what words, names, or ideas they remember.

Finally, direct students to the last paragraph and have them read it. Ask students what stands out in the last paragraph for them.

Then have students respond to four or five questions about the selection. Questions might include:

- What is the selection about?
- When does it take place?
- Who is in it?
- How does the selection end?

Return to the questions and discuss the accuracy of students' predictions. Were they surprised at how the selection turned out based on their initial preview? Why or why not?

Why It Works

Previews work because they provide a frame of reference in which to understand new material. Previews build context, particularly when reading about unfamiliar topics. Discussing the questions and predicting before reading help students set purposes for reading and create interest in the subject matter.

Comments and Cautions

Previews work best with difficult, content-intensive reading selections. Especially with nonfiction and texts with difficult vocabulary, it helps students to understand a context for a selection:—What's the subject? Where's the story located? Who's involved?

Word Web

What It Is

A word web is a prereading activity in which students brainstorm about and make connections to a key concept from the reading material. Word webs work especially well with selections about a specific idea, such as weather.

Here is an example from *Sourcebook*, Grade 2, "Sam's Story":

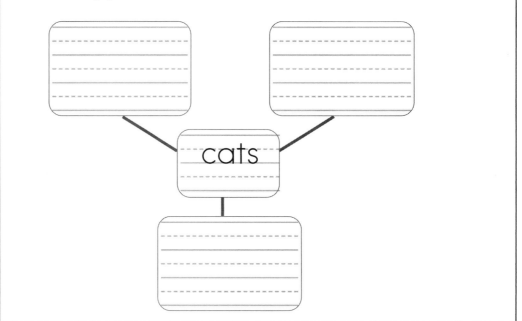

BEFORE YOU READ

Word Web
What do you know about cats? Use the web below to write three things you know about cats.

cats

How to Introduce It

Explain what a word web is. Tell students that you will put a word in the center of the web and you want them to think of as many other words and ideas as they can that connect to that word.

Walk students through the activity as a group. Take a general idea, such as "transportation." Ask students to give examples of transportation. Then ask them how they feel about different kinds of transportation (cars, planes, trains, spaceships, etc.).

After modeling how to complete a web, ask students to complete the one in the *Sourcebook*. Then have them share their webs with two or three other students before reading the selection.

Why It Works

Word webs are excellent tools for developing students' conceptual knowledge. They tap into students' prior knowledge and help students make connections between what they know and what they will learn.

Comments and Cautions

If students get "stuck," encourage them to write down words, phrases, examples, or images they associate with the concept. For this strategy, it is helpful for students to work together in groups. Allow sufficient time for students to experience success as they create ideas about the subject before they start the selection.

ACTIVE READING STRATEGIES

Active Reading Strategies are the heart of the interactive reading students will do throughout the book. In **Part II** of each lesson, students read the selection actively, marking or highlighting the text or writing comments and reactions to it. In one reading, they read and mark. In another reading, they write or draw their thoughts in "My Notes" beside each selection.

To maintain focus, the directions ask readers to do only one thing at a time. First they read and mark. Struggling readers do not naturally interact with a text, so the strategies are limited to four, and each lesson uses one. The intent is to support their development as active readers.

Examples in each lesson model the strategy and make marking up the text a natural, active way for students to read.

Response Strategies

1. Make clear

2. Connect

3. Question

4. Draw

The purpose of the Response Strategies in each lesson is:

1. To help students learn how to mark up a text

2. To help students focus on specific aspects of a text and find the information they need

3. To build lifelong habits by repeating good reading practices

COMPREHENSION STRATEGIES

Stop and Think/Stop and Explain

What It Is

The Stop and Think and Stop and Explain strategies are forms of directed reading. They are designed to guide students' reading of a selection. Directed reading in its purest form consists of a series of steps, including readiness, directed silent reading, comprehension check and discuss, oral rereading, and follow-up activities. In the **_Sourcebook_**, students gain readiness in **Part I**, read silently in **Part II**, and then encounter questions that check their comprehension throughout the selection.

During the **Reread** step at the end of **Part II**, teachers should have students go back through the selection again, reread the selection another time, and respond to the Stop and Think or Stop and Explain questions. Repeated reading of a selection tends to increase reading fluency and recall of details, which improves reading comprehension.

How to Introduce It

For the first selection with Stop and Think/Stop and Explain questions, point out to students the questions placed in the middle of the selection. Have students read the selection using the directions in **Part II.**

Guide them through active reading of the text on the first reading and to responding to the text on a second reading. Then, after all of the students have made it through the selection, ask students to reread. On this reading, ask students to concentrate on the questions in the text. Tell students to answer each question when they come upon it.

Explain to students that these are the kinds of questions they should be asking themselves as they read.

Here is an example from **_Sourcebook_**, Grade 2, Lesson 1, _I Am an Apple:_

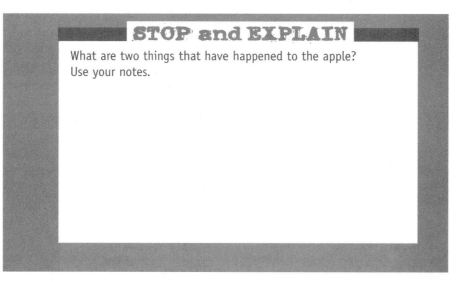

STOP and EXPLAIN

What are two things that have happened to the apple?
Use your notes.

Why It Works

Directed reading helps students ask the questions good readers ask themselves as they read. The structured format of the Stop and Think/Stop and Explain activities ensures that students will be asking the right kinds of questions at the right times in the selection.

Comments and Cautions

Directed reading may need to be modified to fit the needs of individual students. Some students may benefit by answering these questions in groups or by working in pairs.

Directed reading is intended to help students make meaning from the text. Putting the questions in the text may also serve as an interruption of reading for some students. Especially for these students, be sure they read all the way through the selection once before trying to tackle the Stop and Think/Stop and Explain questions.

Stop and Draw

What It Is

Drawing is a comprehension strategy that helps students visualize the story. When they stop to reflect on a reading, they can draw what they imagine has happened.

How to Introduce It

Students probably do not need much introduction to the skill. Explain to them that drawing what they see in their heads will help them remember parts of the reading and might help them figure out the message of the selection.

Here is an example from *Sourcebook,* Grade 2, Lesson 2, *Mice Squeak, We Speak:*

STOP and DRAW

Draw one of the animals in the story.

Comments and Cautions

Many of the selections include illustrations. Make sure students are using their imaginations and not merely copying what they see on the page.

Make the explicit connection for students that, as they read, they should also be making pictures in their heads. If students do not connect their drawing to what they are supposed to be doing while reading, the point will be lost.

Help students see that drawing makes what they read seem "real" and helps them understand what the writer is trying to communicate.

Stop and Retell

What It Is

Retelling is both a comprehension strategy and an assessment tool in which students tell about a selection in their own words. Retelling often works best with chronological stories and as a means of checking that students followed the general "story" in a selection.

How to Introduce It

Introduce retelling as a whole-class activity. For example, you might read a fairy tale out loud or tell the story of the "Billy Goats Gruff" in which three billy goats try to cross a bridge guarded by a troll. First, the small goat meets the troll and persuades him to wait for his bigger brother. Then, the next billy goat meets the troll and persuades the troll to wait for his mother. Then, the mother comes and kicks the troll off the bridge. Ask a volunteer to retell the story. Then ask another volunteer to do so. Explain that retellings will differ somewhat but have the same essential information.

Here is an example from *Sourcebook,* Grade 2, Lesson 4, "Sam's Story":

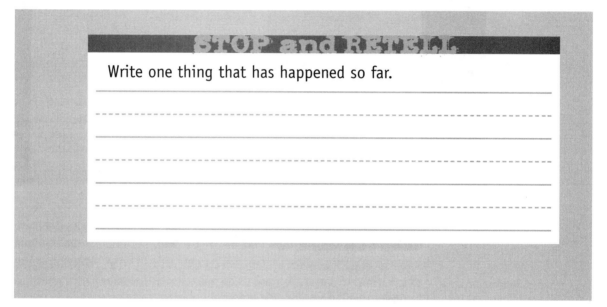

STOP and RETELL

Write one thing that has happened so far.

Why It Works

Explain to students the benefit of retelling as a strategy is that they understand a story better when it is translated into their own words. Mention also that retelling helps them remember the story. Retelling encourages students to make a more personal connection to the text, which makes it more meaningful and promotes a deeper understanding of the material.

Comments and Cautions

Tell students that the goal of a retelling is not to include every detail, but only to tell what is important about the story.

As much as possible, try to make students understand that one retelling is not necessarily better than another simply because it includes more. A retelling should be accurate and reflect the story, no matter what the length.

WORD WORK SKILLS

The notes below outline the strategies included in Word Work sections of the Grade 2 *Sourcebook*. The strategies are listed here to help you reinforce and explicitly teach these ideas (and sometimes rules) about words. Some ideas are taught more than once and get progressively more difficult.

The purpose of the Word Work activities is to help with decoding and ease at-risk readers' stress over reading unknown or long words. Among the ways to help are to show students how to "see" 1) the base word of a long word that might have a prefix, suffix, or both, and that might have undergone a spelling change; 2) smaller words in compound words; 3) syllables; or 4) analogous words. Once students begin to feel comfortable with word recognition strategies, they will be able to decode more words more easily and they will be able to focus on comprehension.

Lesson 1. **Base Words and Adding Suffixes**

One way to add a suffix to a base word is to just add it on.

EXAMPLE: strong + er = stronger

Sometimes the last letter doubles before the suffix.

EXAMPLE: red + d + est = reddest

Lesson 2. **Plurals with *s* or *es***

Words that are plural usually end in *s* or *es*.

EXAMPLES: chicken + s = chickens

wish + es = wishes

Lesson 3. **Adding *y* endings**

Some words add the ending *y* when they describe things. These words are called adjectives.

EXAMPLE: crunch + y = crunchy

Lesson 4. **Adding suffixes**

With words that end in two consonants (talk, dark) or have two vowels that are side by side in the middle (speak, scoop), just add the endings to the word.

EXAMPLE: help + ed = helped

Lesson 5. **Adding *s***

You have learned that you can add *s* to many words to make them plural.

EXAMPLE: coat + s = coats

Lesson 6. **Compound Words**

A compound word is a long word made from two small words.

EXAMPLE: flash + light = flashlight

Lesson 7. Syllables

Words have beats—one, two, three or more beats. Try clapping the word *waterfall*. You clapped three times because *waterfall* has three beats, or syllables.

Some two-syllable words have two consonant letters in the middle. These letters can be the same (bo<u>tt</u>le). These letters can be different (ba<u>sk</u>et, wi<u>nd</u>ow).

Lesson 8. Adding *es* to words with *y*

Some words are made plural by changing a final *y* to *i* and adding *es*.

EXAMPLE: pon + ies = ponies

Lesson 9. Compound Words

You have learned that a compound word is made up of two smaller words.

EXAMPLE: day + time = daytime

Lesson 10. Adding *ed* and *ing*

Some words don't change when adding the suffixes *ed* or *ing*.

EXAMPLE: grow + ing = growing

Lesson 11. Homophones

Words that sound alike but have different spellings are called homophones.

EXAMPLE: buy, by

Lesson 12. Adding *y* or *ly*

Many words do not change when adding the endings *y* or *ly*.

EXAMPLES: soft + ly = softly   dirt + y = dirty

Lesson 13. Contractions

Shortened forms of two combined words are called contractions. An apostrophe replaces the missing letters.

EXAMPLES: I + will = I'll   can + not = can't

Lesson 14. Dividing Words with Two Consonants

Many words have two consonants in the middle of them. Often you can divide these words between the consonants. Example: win/dow. Sometimes you must break the word after the consonants when the consonants together make one sound.

EXAMPLE: mit/ten

To help further with word structure, the Grade 2 *Sourcebook* includes lessons in phonics. Each lesson focuses on a different phonic sound.

WORD WORK ACTIVITIES

To supplement your classroom teaching of word work, try including some of the games described here in your daily classroom routine.

Phonemic and Phonological Awareness

Rhyme Book

Silly Sentences

Odd One Out

Phonics

Word Sorts

Bibliography and Resources

Phonemic and Phonological Awareness

Building phonemic and phonological awareness in students can be a fun, enjoyable activity. You can build this awareness with oral activities. For instance, you may instruct students to repeat the sounds "ac / tor" and then say the word. These activities, however, often seem like drills. An alternative is to create word games that your students can play throughout the school year.

CREATE A RHYME BOOK

Paste one picture from a magazine at the top of a page and label it. For example, you might want to start with short vowels and then move to long vowels, so begin by pasting images for the words *pan, pen, stick, dog*, and *rug* (for short vowels) at the top of different pages. Then have students write other words that know that rhyme with the pictures.

Short *a*   pan

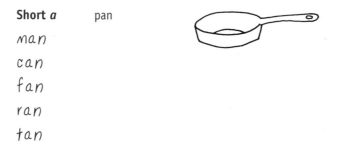

man

can

fan

ran

tan

Then, after working through vowel sounds, have students rhyme common phonograms like *ing*, *ight*, *og*, and so on.

ing words   ring

sing

bring

ring

wing

SILLY SENTENCES

Have students sit in groups of three or four. Then tell them that you need their help to make some silly sentences. As a model, write one or more silly sentences on the board, such as, *Heavy hippos hike high hills*. All words should start with the same letter. Then tell students that one person will begin a new sentence with a word (such as *tiny*), and then ask the person on the left to add another word to make a silly sentence. The first child says, *Tiny*. The next person says something like, *Tiny teddy bears*. The next says, *Tiny teddy bears talk*, and so on until someone ends the sentence or the group cannot think of another word to add.

ODD ONE OUT

Before class, label three big, clear plastic bags **First**, **Middle**, and **End.** Then, using a thick marker, create sets of the words like the ones below. Put a rubber band around each set, and place five to eight sets in each plastic bag.

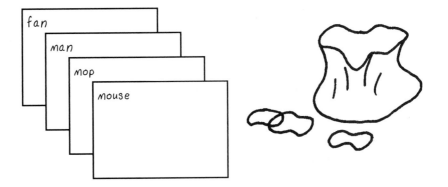

The object is for students to find which word is the "odd one out" in each set of words. They do that by identifying which word sounds different than the other words.

Have students work in groups of three or four. Put them together at a table or on a rug in the corner of the room.

You can ask each student in the group to do one word pack, or you can have the students work together as a group. Have groups trade word packs once they have found the "odd one out." In doing so, they build their phonemic awareness of sounds in English.

EXAMPLE WORD PACKS

Beginning Consonant Sounds

Have students find the words that *begin* with a different consonant.

dog, den, lip, dip

kind, kit, man, kick

fan, man, mop, mouse

Ending Consonant Sounds

Have students find the words that *end* with a different consonant.

dog, log, hip, bag

kid, long, hid, lid

sit, quit, trip, bit

You can also create sets of words to help students discern vowel sounds. Here are some examples of word sets you might create for short vowels and long vowels.

Short Vowels

Have students find the word that has the *different* **short vowel** sound in the middle.

hat, can, top, sat

kid, lid, rug, tin

rock, nod, tent, shop

Long Vowels

Have students find the word that has the *different* **long vowel** sound in the middle.

hope, rake, soap, slope

slide, write, snake, white

seed, lead, line, leap

You can also make packs that focus on rhyming words and on alliteration, both of which will help students develop phonemic awareness.

Rhyming Words

Have students find the sentence that *does not* have rhyming words in it.

Example: The <u>cat</u> met a <u>rat</u>. The <u>frog</u> met a <u>hog</u>. The <u>mouse</u> met a <u>lion</u>.

Alliterative Words

Have students find the sentence that *does not* have alliterative words in it (that is, initial consonant sounds).

Example: Pink pandas pushed pigs. Sunny Sue sang songs. Tiny frogs lived at the zoo.

By using this simple word game at the beginning or end of class, you can make building phonological awareness fun for students. By working with card packs in small groups, you can increase the amount of practice for each student. You also take advantage of students' ability to teach and help each other.

Phonics

For students who need intensive work in phonics, try spending 10–20 minutes of each class building their knowledge. Students need to become attuned to hearing the sounds of English words and letters. They need to develop an understanding of different sounds for different letters (for example, *p* and *d*). They should also know the difference between different sounds (for example, short *u* and *ur*).

Word Sorts

One valuable tool in building students' awareness of phonics is a word sort. You can use the word sort to focus attention on any sound or group of letters that your students need. Word sorts are quick, easy ways for students to work on word sounds.

Word sorts have many benefits. Word sorts are fun group activities in which everyone can participate. Students benefit from the work of their fellow students; they learn without being put on the spot to answer, reducing potential embarrassment.

Word sorts also allow you to emphasize a core of frequently used words and to teach common spelling patterns. With word sorts, you can teach simple phonics concepts as well as complex phonograms, such as *ank, ash, eat, ick, ide, ing,* and *oke.*

Here is an example of a word sort.

Directions:

1. Say the words in the box below. Listen for these short vowel sounds: *a* as in hat; *o* as in chop; and *i* as in trip.

2. Write each word in the box in the column that matches the short vowel sound you hear.

3. Write the other words under "Extra Words."

path	shop	mud
box	dash	pinch
thrill	met	trot
clock	mint	patch
string	block	trap
branch	drift	stilt
up	flash	sock

hat	chop	trip	Extra Words

You can use word sorts to teach phonics in a systematic way across the school year. You can create a series of word sorts week after week with frequently used words. Here are examples of word sorts you can do.

k, c, n, m

kiss	cave	nap	mom
kind	cake	neck	mix
key	cup	nest	moon
kill	carrot	need	mare
king	camp	north	mild

short a, e, o

flag	best	rock
bag	web	box
pack	nest	fox
lamp	red	trot
last	next	mop

long a, e, i

safe	heat	mice
grape	keep	dime
sale	sheet	nice
tail	me	nine
rail	read	find

adding s, es, ing

dogs	glasses	cooking
fences	dresses	drinking
cans	dishes	eating
songs	messes	making
pens	benches	sleeping

adding ed

baked	barked	mopped
signed	lined	hopped
packed	noted	stopped
needed	used	pegged

Bibliography and Resources

Phonemic Awareness Activities for Early Reading Success, by Wily Blevins. New York: Scholastic, 1997.

This book contains easy, entertaining games and activities that teach children phonics and phonemic awareness. Games involving familiar activities like board games and singing will appeal to students.

Phonics They Use: Words for Reading and Writing by Patricia M. Cunningham. New York: Longman, 2000.

Cunningham explains the fundamentals of teaching phonics to young children and then provides specific activities for the classroom.

Systematic Sequential Phonics They Use: For Beginning Readers of Any Age by Patricia M. Cunningham. Greensboro, NC: Carson-Dellosa, 2000.

In this book, Cunningham has written 140 lessons that teach common phonics patterns. Because the lessons increase in difficulty, starting with short vowels and moving on to more complex phonics, teachers can easily include this book in their lesson plan.

Making Words: Multilevel, Hands-On, Developmentally Appropriate Spelling and Phonics Activities by Patricia M. Cunningham and Dorothy P. Hall. Torrance, CA: Good Apple, 1994.

This book focuses on spelling skills. Each page lists several letters, which teachers and students can combine in different ways to make several words. These "making words" activities will provide a good foundation for phonics and spelling skills.

The Teacher's Guide to the Four Blocks®: A Multimethod, Multilevel Framework for Grades 1–3 by Patricia M. Cunningham, Dorothy P. Hall, and Cheryl M. Sigman. Greensboro, NC: Carson-Dellosa, 1999.

This is a guide to the Four Blocks® system of instruction. With relevant activities for the four sections (guided reading, self-selected reading, writing, and working with words), this book shows how word work fits into your larger lesson plan.

Word Matters: Teaching Phonics and Spelling in the Reading/Writing Classroom by Gay Su Pinnell and Irene C. Fountas. Portsmouth, NH: Heinemann, 1998.

Pinnell and Fountas have written an extremely comprehensive guide on how to develop phonics and spelling programs. This book includes an explanation of theories and specific activities to teach students.

i Am an Apple

BACKGROUND

Jean Marzollo's descriptive *I Am an Apple* is the story of a plant that grows from a small bud into an apple ready to be picked. Along the way, it goes through several colorful stages of growth.

I Am an Apple, part of the "Hello Reader! Science" series, explains the growing cycle of an apple from the perspective of the fruit itself. With its simple presentation of a scientific process, this selection will surprise and interest students. Collages further illustrate the concepts.

BIBLIOGRAPHY Students might enjoy reading another science book by Jean Marzollo. Set up a small classroom library of her works, many of which students will be able to read independently. Think about including the following: *I Am a Rock*, *I Am a Leaf*, and *I Am Fire*.

(Lexile 70)

(Lexile 70)

(Lexile 160)

How to Introduce the Reading

i Am an Apple
By Jean Marzollo

What do you know about apples?

Where have you seen apples?

What color is each apple? Write the colors below.

Direct students' attention to the opening page of *I Am an Apple* (student book page 5). Pique students' interest in the reading to come by asking, *How many of you have eaten an apple in the last day? What did it taste like?* Then explain that the story they're about to read tells about a plant growing into the fruit that they eat. Ask if any of the students have eaten an apple that they picked themselves.

Other Reading

Read aloud other science books written at this same reading level. There are many good books available, including these three:

ELEPHANTS
by
Shirleyann
Costigan

(Lexile 130)

WIND AND SUN
by John Parker

(Lexile 100)

THE VERY HUNGRY
CATERPILLAR
by Eric Carle

(Lexile 460)

I Am an Apple

Skills and Strategies Overview

PREREADING	predict and preview
READING LEVEL	Lexile 120
RESPONSE	stop and explain
VOCABULARY	◇bud ◇branch ◇stem ◇blossom ◇petals ◇beautiful
COMPREHENSION	draw
WORD WORK	short *a*
MORE WORD WORK	suffixes
WRITING	sentence

OTHER RESOURCES

The first **four** pages of this teacher's lesson describe Parts I–IV of the lesson. Also included are the following **six** blackline masters. Use them to reinforce key elements of the lesson.

Vocabulary

Prereading

Comprehension

Word Work

More Word Work

Assessment

1. BEFORE YOU READ

Activate prior knowledge and generate interest in the reading to come by asking students to think about their favorite fruits. Have them imagine where the food came from. Work together to create a list of places where we find food. Then assign the prereading activity, making predictions. (Refer to the Strategy Handbook on page 43 for more help on predicting.)

Motivation Strategy

CONNECTING WITH STUDENTS Ask students to talk about plants they have seen around their homes and the school. Examine a classroom plant, if possible, and talk about how plants grow from seeds. Help students make a connection between some of the food they eat and the plants around them.

Studying Words

VOCABULARY STRATEGIES Use the Studying Words activity on page 64 as a kind of vocabulary pretest. Spot check for difficulties with pronunciation, spelling, and definitions. Explain that some of the stories in the *Sourcebook* will contain words that are unfamiliar to students. Discuss strategies students might use when they come to a difficult word. Good vocabulary strategies include:

- Stop, sound, say
- Guess and go
- Look for context clues
- Consult a vocabulary journal, glossary, or dictionary

Then help students label a diagram with simple plant parts: stem, blossom, and so on.

For prereading vocabulary work, use the **Studying Words** blackline master on page 64.

Prereading Strategies

PREVIEW For their first prereading activity, students will **preview** the text for a sense of what the story is about. Instruct students that previewing means turning the pages of the book one at a time and looking at the pictures and text both. You'll want to explain, however, that previewing is *not* reading. Rather, it is allowing your eyes to "catch" on words and art that seem interesting or important. Familiarizing themselves with the text ahead of time can make it easier for students to complete their careful readings. Use the top half of the Before You Read page (student book page 6) to support this activity.

PREDICT After they preview *I Am an Apple,* students will be able to make some thoughtful **predictions** about the text. Ask, *What do you think this story is about? What do you think will be the most interesting parts?* As you know, making predictions can generate interest in the reading to come, while at the same time provide students with a purpose for reading. Explain to students that one of the reasons they'll read *I Am an Apple* is to find out if their predictions actually come true. Use the bottom half of the Before You Read page (student book page 6) to support this activity.

If you feel students need additional practice, assign the **Before You Read** blackline master on page 65.

MY PURPOSE Establishing a purpose for reading will help students maintain their focus and make it easier for them to find essential details in the text. To clarify what it means to set a purpose, direct students to turn to page 6 of the *Sourcebook*. Have a volunteer read aloud the purpose question. Then explain to students that they'll be reading for an answer to this question. Finish by telling students that some of the during-reading notes they make should relate to this purpose question.

II. READ

Response Strategy

FIRST READING Before students begin their initial reading, explain the purpose of **visualizing.** Direct students' attention to the two "Stop and Explain" boxes that interrupt the text. Explain that these boxes are there to help students understand the events of the story. Also be sure to point out the "My Notes" area on each page. Invite students to use this area for sketches as well as for their notes.

Comprehension Strategy

SECOND READING Remind students that good readers try to do at least two readings of a story. On the second reading the reader can look for details he or she missed the first time around. It's also an opportunity to write additional "My Notes" and to find specific words or phrases that relate to the reading purpose.

Assign the **Comprehension** blackline master on page 66 as a way of furthering students' understanding of the story.

Discussion Questions

COMPREHENSION 1. What is the plant like at the beginning? *(The apple starts as a red bud.)*

2. What else happens to the plant before it is an apple? *(It is a blossom.)*

3. What happens at the end? *(The apple is ready to be picked.)*

CRITICAL THINKING 4. What makes the apple grow? *(Possible: Rain, sun, food, and water all make the apple grow.)*

5. What surprised you about *I Am an Apple*? *(Answers will vary. Possible: I was surprised that apples can change color.)*

Reread

THIRD READING If you find that students are struggling with the Discussion Questions above, instruct them to do one more reading. Tell them that they can look for the answers to the questions. Then ask students to discuss what they learned from the text and what they saw in the art. Ask, *What does the plant look like in this picture?*

Word Work

SHORT A Students need to learn that words are made of sounds. Use the first Word Work lesson on student book page 12 to boost students' understanding of the **short a** sound. As a class, brainstorm words that contain short *a*, including: *cap, map, rat,* and *ant.* Say each word sound by sound. /c/ /a/ /p/ Then check to see if students can differentiate short *a* from other short vowel sounds and long *a*. Ask, *What sound do you hear in* mat? *What vowel sound do you hear in* light? *What about* tap *and* tape? When you feel students are ready, assign the **Word Work** lesson on their own.

Assign the **Word Work** blackline master on page 67 if you feel students need additional practice with short *a*.

More Word Work

ADDING ER AND EST Use the second Word Work lesson on student book page 13 to offer students practice in adding *er* and *est* suffixes. Walk students through the activity before you ask them to complete it on their own. First, read the directions aloud. Then read the examples slowly and carefully while students follow along. Finish by having students complete the activity.

Assign the **More Word Work** blackline master on page 68 if you feel students need more practice writing words with *er* or *est*.

III. WRITE

DRAW Use the prewriting activity at the top of student book page 14 to prepare your students for the assignment to come: Write a sentence about apples using descriptive words. Before students begin their drawings, discuss the kinds of words that might be called "describing" words. Have students return to the selection and find examples of adjectives. Students might suggest *red, green,* or *beautiful.*

WRITE A SENTENCE After students complete their group work, assign the bottom half of the Draw and Write page (student book page 14). Read the directions aloud to students and be sure they understand that their assignment is to write a **sentence** about apples. The sentence they write should contain a "describing" word, possibly one of the ones they used for their drawings. Finish your instructions by brainstorming the characteristics of a sentence. Explain to the class that a sentence is a group of words that states a complete thought. A sentence begins with a capital letter and ends with a punctuation mark.

Post an incomplete sentence and a complete sentence on the board.
ran away   I went shopping. Discuss the difference.

After students finish writing, have them reread their work to be sure they've included a describing word in their sentence.

WRITING RUBRIC Use this rubric to help with a quick assessment of students' writing.

Do students' sentences

- begin with a capital letter and end with a punctuation mark?

- express a complete thought?

Grammar, Usage, and Mechanics

Create a Writer's Checklist on the board to which students can refer as they edit their work. Checklist items include:

✔ My sentence begins with a capital letter.

✔ My sentence ends with a punctuation mark.

✔ My sentence tells a complete thought.

IV. LOOK BACK

Reflect with students on their enjoyment of *I Am an Apple.* Invite students to name their favorite parts of the story and explain their choices.

To test students' comprehension of the material, use the **Lesson Test** blackline master on page 69.

Name _____

STUDYING WORDS

Before Reading

DIRECTIONS Look at this picture of a plant.

Then label the picture using words from the word box.

> petal   stem   bud   blossom

Name _____

BEFORE YOU READ

Picture Walk

DIRECTIONS Take a picture walk through *I Am an Apple*.

Look at every picture.

Then answer these questions.

My Picture Walk of *I Am an Apple*

1. Which picture did you like the best? Tell why.

_____

_____

2. What did you learn about apples from the pictures?

_____

_____

3. What do you predict the story will be about?

_____

_____

Name _____

COMPREHENSION

Story String

DIRECTIONS Complete this Story String to tell what happens in *I Am an Apple*. Use the words or phrases to tell what happens.

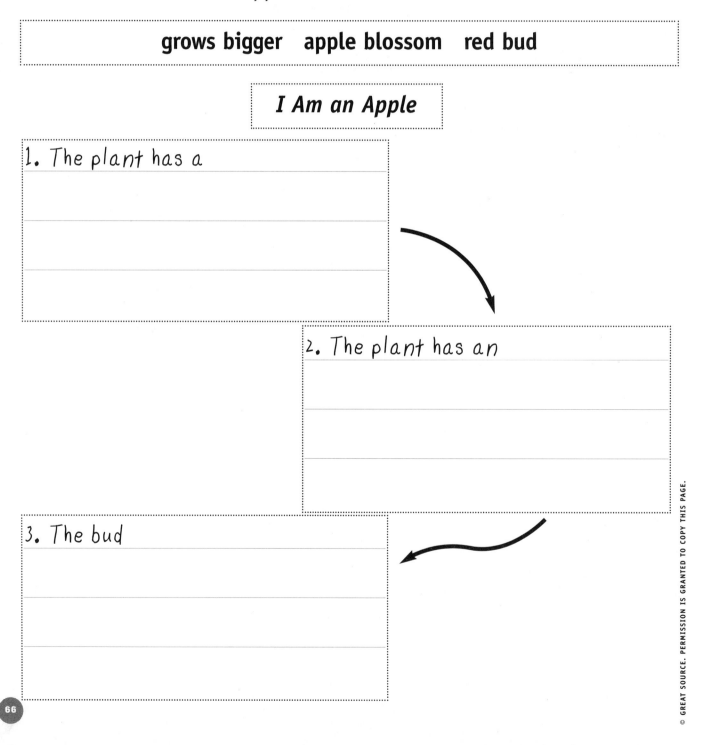

grows bigger   apple blossom   red bud

I Am an Apple

1. The plant has a

2. The plant has an

3. The bud

Name _____

WORD WORK

Short a Sound

DIRECTIONS Read this rhyme. Circle five words that have the short *a* sound.

Rhyme

This is the story of a happy man.

He took a swing at bat.

But he lost his hat.

Practice

DIRECTIONS Write the words from the list that have the short *a* sound.

| mop | nap | flop | flag | at | red | rat | rug |

1. _____

2. _____

3. _____

4. _____

Name _____

MORE WORD WORK

Adding er *or* est

DIRECTIONS Find the words with suffixes in these sentences. Circle the suffixes.

1. I gave my sister the biggest piece of the cake.

2. Joe can jump higher than Mark.

3. Today is the coldest day of the year.

Practice

DIRECTIONS Add suffixes to these words to make new words. Write the new words on the lines.

1. tall + est = _____

2. dark + er = _____

3. mad + d + er = _____

4. slow + est = _____

Name _____

LESSON TEST

Multiple-Choice

DIRECTIONS Write the letter of the best answer for each question on the line.

_____ 1. What color is the bud?

    A. green   C. yellow

    B. red   D. white

_____ 2. Rain and _____ make the plant grow.

    A. snow   C. wind

    B. salt   D. sun

_____ 3. How many petals does the blossom have?

    A. ten   C. five

    B. two   D. four

_____ 4. The apple is ready to be picked when it is_____.

    A. red   C. pink

    B. orange   D. white

Short Answer

What step comes next for the apple? Write your answer below.

_____

_____

Mice Squeak, We Speak

BACKGROUND

Arnold L. Shapiro's easy-to-read *Mice Squeak, We Speak* is a good introduction to the noises different animals make. Some of these animals will be familiar to students, while some may be new to them. Shapiro's text lists the animals with pleasing repetition, conveying the message to children that different animals make different sounds. Samples of Tomie dePaola's colorful illustrations also appear in the *Sourcebook.*

Students would enjoy Shapiro's entire book, as every statement has its own illustration. If there's time, find a copy of the book in your local library. Let students explore the art for inspiration for their own drawings.

BIBLIOGRAPHY Students might enjoy reading other books about animals. The following books all have Lexile ratings that are close to the rating assigned to *Mice Squeak, We Speak.*

DEER AT THE BROOK by Jim Arnosky

(Lexile 50)

AT THE ZOO by Elizabeth Apgar

(Lexile 40)

MY DOG RUSTY by Katherine Broomfield

(Lexile 50)

How to Introduce the Reading

Use the visualizing activity on student book page 15 as a way of introducing the book to students. As you know, visualizing can generate interest and prompt students to become more active readers. Begin the activity by explaining that students are about to read a book about different animals. Ask the class, *What animals do you see every day? What are your favorite animals?* Then read aloud the directions at the top of page 15. Encourage students to use crayons or markers as a way of making their pictures more vivid. If possible, have them write the name of the animal or animals they drew at the bottom of the page.

Other Reading

Show or read aloud to students other books about the natural world. The following three texts hold tremendous kid appeal and should be easy enough for independent reading. All three have a Lexile score of BR (*Beginning Reading*).

(Lexile Beginning Reading)

(Lexile Beginning Reading)

(Lexile Beginning Reading)

Mice Squeak, We Speak

STUDENT PAGES 15–24

Skills and Strategies Overview

PREREADING	preview
READING LEVEL	Lexile 60
RESPONSE	question
VOCABULARY	✦ owls ✦ crickets ✦ doves ✦ coyotes ✦ parrots
COMPREHENSION	draw
WORD WORK	short *u*
MORE WORD WORK	adding *s* and *es*
WRITING	sentence

OTHER RESOURCES

The first **four** pages of this teacher's lesson describe Parts I–IV of the lesson. Also included are these **six** blackline masters. Use them to reinforce key elements of the lesson.

Vocabulary

Prereading

Comprehension

Word Work

More Word Work

Assessment

1. BEFORE YOU READ

After students finish their prereading drawings, invite volunteers to share their work with the class. Ask students to comment on the variety of animals their classmates drew. Invite them to decide which animals they'd most like to read about and perhaps make predictions about the types of animals they're going to see in Shapiro's story. After you finish your discussion, direct their attention to the Before You Read activity on student book page 16.

Motivation Strategy

MOTIVATING STUDENTS Have students explore their personal feelings about animals. Take them outside and have them search the schoolyard for animals of interest. If you like, have students bring their notebooks so that they can make notes and drawings of what they see.

Studying Words

CONTEXT CLUES Use the Studying Words activity on student book page 17 to troubleshoot vocabulary problems students may have while reading *Mice Squeak, We Speak*. Review how to add *s* or *es* to a word to make it plural. After students work their way through the page, you might decide to teach a short vocabulary lesson on using **context clues** to understand the meaning of unknown words.

VOCABULARY To begin the lesson, show students these vocabulary words in *Mice Squeak, We Speak*: *owls, crickets, doves, coyotes,* and *parrots*. Explain that because these animals might not be as familiar as the others, students might have to use context clues or look up the words somewhere else. At the prereading or beginning reading level, students will benefit from using the book's artwork as clues to the meaning of some of the words, such as *owls* and *doves*.

To extend the activity, use the **Studying Words** blackline master on page 76.

Prereading Strategies

PREVIEW Students will **preview** *Mice Squeak, We Speak* as a prereading activity. Read aloud the directions at the top of the page. Then discuss each item in the Preview Checklist. Ask, *Why is it important to preview the title of a book or story? Why is it important to look at the first and last sentences?* Then direct students to begin previewing. Have them check off items as they thumb through the selection. When they've finished, instruct students to note what they saw on their previews. Doing so will make the text feel "familiar"—and thus easier to understand. (Refer to the Strategy Handbook on page 43 for more help on previewing.)

CONCEPT MAP As an additional prereading activity, invite students to make a **concept map** that explores their thoughts and feelings about their favorite animal. Have them use the following prompts to discuss their ideas about this animal:

What it is . . .

Where it lives . . .

How it makes me feel . . .

When students finish their concept maps, invite them to share with the class. Use the activity as a way of helping students make a strong personal connection to the text they're about to read.

To extend the activity, use the **Before You Read** blackline master on page 77.

MY PURPOSE Read aloud the purpose statement on student book page 16. Be sure students understand that you'd like them to think about what the animals look like as they read. Invite them to look at the animals in the illustrations as well as think about the ones they've seen in real life.

READ

Response Strategy

FIRST READING Before students begin their first readings, explain the response strategy of asking during-reading **questions.** Point out the example in the "My Notes" on page 18. Explain that "What does a hoot sound like?" is a question one reader has about the story. Tell the class, *Your questions about the story may be different from those of your neighbor. That's because every reader has his or her own ideas about a story. No one reads a story in exactly the same way. So, no one will make exactly the same during-reading notes.* Then read aloud the first and second pages of *Mice Squeak, We Speak.* Pause while students record their questions. Later, you'll want to come together as a group to discuss their questions.

Comprehension Strategy

SECOND READING Be sure students understand that as they are reading Shapiro's book, they will need to stop occasionally in order to **draw** something in the text. On pages 19 and 21, there are spaces for them to draw animals. Keep in mind that pausing in the middle of a reading to respond to the text can help readers more effectively process what they've read. Explain to the class that the notes they make in the Stop and Explain areas are for their eyes only—meaning, you won't be grading them. When it comes to the interrupter text, students should feel free to give their gut reactions to what they're reading and not be distracted by concerns about proper spelling, punctuation, and so on.

For more help with **Comprehension,** assign the blackline master on page 78.

Discussion Questions

COMPREHENSION
1. What noise do lions make? *(they roar)*

2. What animals make the sound "moo"? *(cows)*

3. Who is Arnold L. Shapiro? *(He is the author of* Mice Squeak, We Speak.)

CRITICAL THINKING
4. If someone asked you to tell what *Mice Squeak, We Speak* is about, what would you say? *(Answers will vary. Possible: It tells about the noises that different animals make.)*

5. What is the main idea of *Mice Squeak, We Speak?* *(Answers will vary. Possible: Animals and people all make their own noises.)*

Reread

THIRD READING When they reread, students may still not know some of the animals. Have volunteers look up the names of unfamiliar animals in a student dictionary. Find pictures of them on the Internet.

Word Work

SHORT U Use the first Word Work lesson on student book page 22 to improve students' ability to hear the **short *u*** vowel sound in one-syllable words. In addition, use the lesson to help students learn to differentiate between short *u* and vowels that sound similar—especially short *o*. When they finish the lesson, check to be sure that they've listed *cluck, buzz,* and *but* on the left-hand side of the chart. Offer additional words to sort if you feel they need the practice.

For additional practice, see the **Word Work** blackline master on page 79.

More Word Work

PLURALS WITH S Use the second Word Work lesson on student book page 23 to offer students practice in **creating *s* plurals.** Begin by explaining that a plural shows more than one person, place, or thing. Tell the class: *Most of the time, you can make a word plural by adding either* s *or* es. *Words ending in* sh, ch, s, ss, *and* x *add* es. *For example, the plural of* bug *is* bugs, *and the plural of* dish *is* dishes. Then write the following singular nouns on the board and ask volunteers to make them plural:

lock   class   dog   inch   book   box

Finish the lesson by reading aloud the directions on page 23 and asking students to complete the page either on their own or with a partner.

Assign the **More Word Work** blackline master on page 80 if you feel students need more practice making plurals with *s* and *es*.

III. WRITE

DRAW Use the drawing activity at the top of student book page 24 as a kind of prewriting exercise. Invite students to use as much detail as they can in drawing their favorite "animal place." As they complete their drawings, students should think about why they like this place. When they've finished, have them get together into small groups and share their work. Ask each group member to show his or her art and then tell what the place is like. Be sure they discuss the kinds and numbers of animals they see in the place they've drawn.

WRITE A SENTENCE After students complete their group work, assign the bottom half of the Draw and Write page (page 24). Read the directions aloud to students and be sure they understand that their assignment is to write a **sentence** about the animal place they drew. Students should use plural words if they drew more than one animal. Finish your instructions by brainstorming the characteristics of a sentence. Remind the class that a sentence is a group of words that states something. A sentence begins with a capital letter and ends with a punctuation mark.

WRITING RUBRIC Use this rubric to help with a quick assessment of students' writing.

Do students' sentences

• begin with a capital letter and end with a punctuation mark?

• express a complete thought?

• use plural words correctly?

Grammar, Usage, and Mechanics

Before students proofread their work, teach a brief lesson on end punctuation. Remind the class that a sentence can end with a period, an exclamation mark, or a question mark. Also discuss how to choose the correct end punctuation. For example, ask, *What end punctuation do you use with a question? What end punctuation do you use with a statement?*

IV. LOOK BACK

End the lesson by discussing the ease or difficulty with which students read the Shapiro selection. What made it easy for them to read? What made it challenging?

To test students' comprehension, use the **Lesson Test** blackline master on page 81.

Name _____

STUDYING WORDS

Before Reading

DIRECTIONS Read the word box.

Then choose a word to complete each thought.

doves parrots owls coyotes crickets

1. _____ are white birds that fly.

2. Bugs that chirp are _____ .

3. We saw two hooting _____ high in a tree.

4. _____ look like big dogs and howl.

5. Birds with bright colors are _____ .

Practice

Write another sentence that tells something about *parrots*.

_____

Name _____

BEFORE YOU READ

Concept Web

DIRECTIONS Write words about mice on this web.

Then record your ideas about mice below.

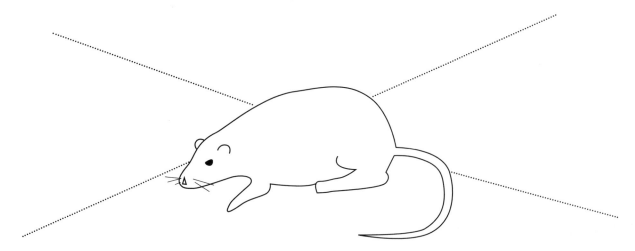

Mice _____

What they are . . . _____

What they are not . . . _____

Where I see them . . . _____

How I feel about them . . . _____

Name _____

COMPREHENSION

Questions

DIRECTIONS Answer these questions about animals. Look back at the story if you need help.

1. What noise do sheep make?

2. What animals coo?

3. What animals croak?

Practice

DIRECTIONS Draw a picture of your favorite animal sleeping.

Name _____

WORD WORK

Short u Sound

DIRECTIONS Complete each word using a vowel from the box. Write the vowel on the line.

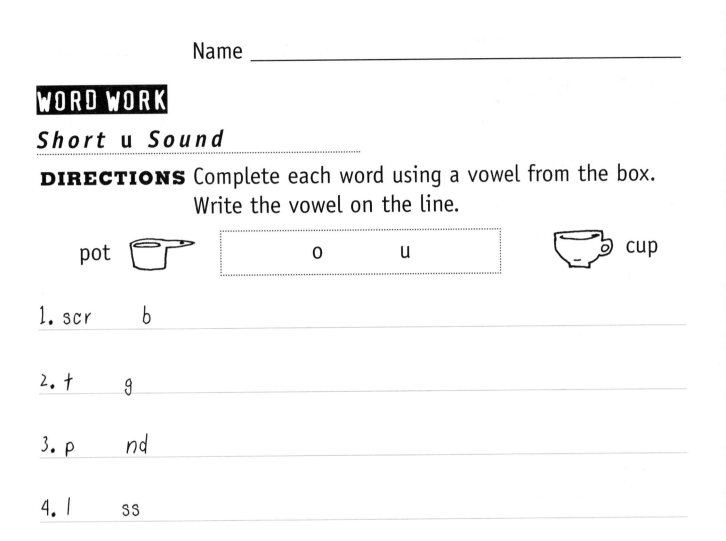

pot

| o | u |

cup

1. scr __ b

2. t __ g

3. p __ nd

4. l __ ss

Practice

DIRECTIONS Write three words from the box that have the same short *u* sound you hear in *bug*.

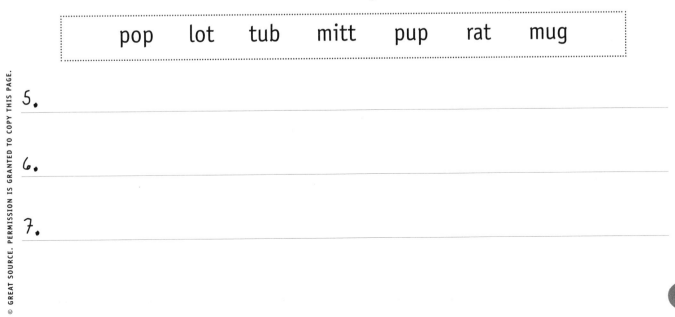

| pop | lot | tub | mitt | pup | rat | mug |

5. _____

6. _____

7. _____

Name _____

MORE WORD WORK

Plurals with s and es

DIRECTIONS Read the words in the word box.

Make each word a plural by adding *s* or *es*.

Write the new word in the correct place on the chart.

rat bear fan	dish class box

Making Plurals

Add *s*   **Add *es***

1.   1.

2.   2.

3.   3.

Practice

DIRECTIONS Now think of two plural words on your own.

Make one an *s* plural and one an *es* plural.

Write them on the lines.

1.   2.

Name _____

LESSON TEST

Multiple-Choice

DIRECTIONS Write the letter of the best answer for each question on the line.

_____ 1. Which of these things doesn't make a noise?

A. cricket   C. grass

B. parrot   D. cat

_____ 2. What animal growls the most?

A. cow   C. cat

B. horse   D. dog

_____ 3. Only _____ speak.

A. people   C. pigs

B. horses   D. ducks

_____ 4. An important idea in *Mice Squeak, We Speak* is this.

A. All animals sleep.

B. Animals make different noises.

C. Animals are too loud.

D. Animals are funny.

Short Answer

Write a sentence that tells about a noise an animal makes sometimes.

_____

_____

Bread, Bread, Bread

BACKGROUND

Bread, Bread, Bread is nonfiction author Ann Morris's fascinating look at breads of the world—tacos, pitas, crackers, bagels, tortillas, baguettes, and many others—and the children and adults who enjoy them. Morris keeps her text simple enough for young children to read, although her message—that people of the world have so much in common—is one that adults will benefit from hearing as well. You'll find that students in your reading class will want to return to Morris's book again and again over the course of the year. You'll notice, too, that the **Sourcebook** excerpt from *Bread, Bread, Bread* can dovetail nicely with a social studies unit on community values.

The talented Ann Morris, an author, editor, and former teacher, has written several books for children, including *Families; Hats, Hats, Hats; On the Go;* and *Loving.* She is also the author of *Shoes, Shoes, Shoes,* which is reprinted in part on pages 49–58 of the **Sourcebook**.

Morris has traveled the world to conduct research and is endlessly fascinated by what she has seen and learned. Clearly, one of her goals as a writer is to convey that knowledge—and fascination—to children and adults alike.

BIBLIOGRAPHY Students might enjoy reading another book by Ann Morris. The three books shown below have approximately the same reading level as *Bread, Bread, Bread* (Lexile 30).

(Lexile 30)   (Lexile Beginning Reading)   (Not rated)

How to Introduce the Reading

The opening activity for *Bread, Bread, Bread* (student book page 25) is an anticipation guide. To complete the activity, students will respond to four questions and then draw a picture about bread. Keep in mind that anticipation guides serve two important purposes:

1. They help activate prior knowledge about a topic, which in turn makes the selection easier to read.

2. They provide students with a clear-cut purpose for reading and can serve as a guide for the key details students must search for as they read.

After students finish their anticipation guide, discuss their responses. If there is disagreement, allow students to debate the question, although consensus may not be possible at this point.

When students finish reading *Bread, Bread, Bread,* have them return to page 25 to see how their answers have changed. This quick activity can help prove to students that we really *do* learn things from a text.

Other Reading

Students may enjoy listening as you read aloud other books from around the world. The following three have food or cooking as a topic:

(Lexile AD690)   (Lexile 500)   (Lexile Beginning Reading)

Bread, Bread, Bread

Skills and Strategies Overview

PREREADING K-W-L

READING LEVEL Lexile 30

RESPONSE make personal connections

VOCABULARY ✧people ✧crunchy ✧soak ✧pizza ✧pretzel

COMPREHENSION web

WORD WORK short *a*

MORE WORD WORK adding *y* endings

WRITING sentence

OTHER RESOURCES

The first **four** pages of this teacher's lesson describe Parts I–IV of the lesson. Also included are these **six** blackline masters. Use them to reinforce key elements of the lesson.

Vocabulary

Prereading

Comprehension

Word Work

More Word Work

Assessment

BEFORE YOU READ

After students finish their anticipation guides, invite volunteers to share their work with the class. Read each statement aloud and have students raise their hands to vote "yes" or "no." Then direct the class to complete another prereading activity—the K-W-L on student book page 26.

Motivation Strategy

MOTIVATING STUDENTS Have students name and then describe their favorite type of bread. Encourage students to discuss breads from other cultures and what certain ones taste like. Make a list on the board of the breads they name and explain to students that you'd like them to keep an eye out for additional types of bread as they read.

Studying Words

PREDICT AND GO Use the Studying Words activity on student book page 27 to introduce students to words with *ing* endings. Encourage students to think of more than five *ing* words if possible, or brainstorm an additional list of words as a group. Then teach a short lesson on the vocabulary strategy **predict and go** as a way of preparing students for their careful readings.

The strategy of predict and go teaches students that not all words are worth stopping for—and puzzling over—especially on an initial reading. Explain that when using this strategy, students will read for overall meaning first and leave text-level problems for later.

Of course, predict and go doesn't work quite as well as a vocabulary strategy if students come to a word that *is* essential to the meaning of a sentence. Explain that when this happens—when they can't figure out what a sentence is saying because they don't know the meaning of a certain word—students should search for context clues in surrounding sentences.

Finish your vocabulary lesson by posting the following words from *Bread, Bread, Bread* on the board: *people, crunchy, soak, pizza,* and *pretzel.* Ask volunteers for a definition of each. Explain to students that they'll get more from their reading of *Bread, Bread, Bread* if they understand beforehand what these key words mean.

Prereading Strategies

K-W-L Direct students to turn to student book page 26. Read the directions at the top of the **K-W-L** page. Be sure students understand the purpose of the *K* column, the purpose of the *W* column, and the purpose of the *L* column. This activity offers students a chance to think about what they know about bread, and—more important—what they'd like to find out. Like an Anticipation Guide, a K-W-L can help students get a handle on the details they should look for in the reading to come.

PICTURE WALK As an additional prereading activity, have students complete a **picture walk** of *Bread, Bread, Bread.* Ask them to thumb through the pages of the text, paying special attention to the different types of bread shown. Then ask, *What breads did you see? What people did you see? What are the people doing and where do they live?* After their picture walks, invite students to write down their predictions about the text.

Use the **Before You Read** blackline master on page 89 to support this activity.

MY PURPOSE Students' purpose for reading the *Sourcebook* excerpt of *Bread, Bread, Bread* will be to find out about different kinds of bread. Ask the class to watch for details about various types of bread and places in the world in which each type is eaten.

READ

Response Strategy

FIRST READING   Before they begin, direct students' attention to the "My Notes" section on student book page 28. Read aloud the comment one reader made about the text. Explain that, in this case, the reader was able to **connect** to something in Morris's book. Invite students to use a highlighter to mark specific words or phrases that they think are interesting or meaningful. Then, in "My Notes," they should write what the text reminds them of in their own lives. These types of connections can help readers process information and remember what they've learned.

Comprehension Strategy

SECOND READING   After they finish reading *Bread, Bread, Bread,* students will be asked to write words that describe bread. This activity will prepare them for writing.

For more help with **Comprehension,** assign the blackline master on page 90.

Discussion Questions

COMPREHENSION   1. What is the title of the selection? *(Bread, Bread, Bread)*

2. What different shapes does bread come in? *(It comes in all different shapes: round, square, flat, triangular, rectangular, and so on. See how many shapes students can name.)*

CRITICAL THINKING   3. Is the selection fiction or nonfiction? *(Nonfiction. If students are struggling with this question, review the differences between fiction and nonfiction.)*

4. What kinds of bread are popular in the United States? *(Answers will vary. Possible: White bread, wheat bread, tacos, bagels, pita.)*

5. What kind of bread would you most like to try? *(Answers will vary. Encourage students to explain their responses.)*

6. What is the main idea of *Bread, Bread, Bread*? *(Possible: People all over the world eat bread.)*

Reread

THIRD READING   Good readers know that it's very difficult, if not impossible, to take in everything on a first reading. Help your students get into the habit of rereading by asking them to reread a work a second and even a third time. On a second and third reading, students can watch for details they missed the first time around. In addition, they can use the time to add to or modify their notes as needed.

Word Work

SHORT A   The first Word Work lesson on student book page 32 is intended to strengthen students' understanding of **short a** and its use in one-syllable words. When students finish the lesson, check to be sure they've circled *cap, bat,* and *man* and that they've marked the *a* in each of the four words at the bottom of the page.

For additional practice, see the **Word Work** blackline master on page 91.

More Word Work

ADDING Y ENDINGS Use the second Word Work lesson on page 33 to offer students practice with **y endings.** Begin by reading aloud the directions at the top of the page. Discuss in particular the meaning of *adjective.* Then return to the selection as a class and watch for the first adjective with a *y* ending that appears: *skinny.* Have students work in pairs to find the remaining *y* adjectives (*crunchy* and *lunchy*).

Assign the **More Word Work** blackline master on page 92 if you feel students need more practice with *y* endings.

III. WRITE

WEB To begin, students will complete a **web** (student book page 34) that explores their knowledge of bread and various words that can be used to describe it. Encourage them to return to the text as often as they like when completing the web and to check the during-reading notes they made for possible words. When the class has finished, draw a large web on the board. To complete this group web have students suggest words from the story and words of their own. Keep the web on the board so that students can refer to it when it comes time to write their sentences.

WRITE A SENTENCE After the class has finished brainstorming, assign the bottom half of the Draw and Write page (page 34). Read the directions aloud to students and be sure they understand that their assignment is to write a **sentence** telling what they learned about bread. The sentence they write should contain at least one adjective from their word webs. Finish your instructions by reviewing the characteristics of a sentence. Remind the class that a sentence is a group of words that states a complete thought. A sentence begins with a capital letter and ends with a punctuation mark.

After students finish writing, have them reread their work to be sure they've included at least one adjective in their sentence.

WRITING RUBRIC Use this rubric to help with a quick assessment of students' writing.

Do students' sentences

- begin with a capital letter and end with a punctuation mark?

- express a complete thought?

- include at least one adjective that describes bread?

Grammar, Usage, and Mechanics

Before students proofread their work, teach a brief lesson on complete sentences. Begin by posting several incomplete sentences on the board. For example:

went to the store   *my older sister*   *Joe and Ali*

Then ask students to explain what's wrong with the sentences. Remind the class that a sentence must express a complete thought. Have three volunteers add words to finish the sentences you've posted on the board.

IV. LOOK BACK

End the lesson by discussing Morris's work and what it means. Help students see that her main idea is expressed in the first sentence of her story: "People eat bread all over the world."

To test students' comprehension, use the **Lesson Test** blackline master on page 93.

Name _____

STUDYING WORDS

Before Reading

DIRECTIONS Add *ing* to each word in the box.

Write the words you make on the lines.

Word Box

round	eat	grow	look	teach

1. _____

2. _____

3. _____

4. _____

5. _____

Practice

Write a statement about bread. Use one of your new words.

_____

Name _____

BEFORE YOU READ

Picture Walk

DIRECTIONS Do a picture walk of *Bread, Bread, Bread*.

Answer these questions.

Then make a prediction about the story.

Picture Walk

1. What kinds of bread did you see? _____

_____

2. What people did you see? _____

_____

3. What are the people in the pictures doing? _____

_____

My Prediction

I think <u>Bread, Bread, Bread</u> will be about _____

_____

Name _____

COMPREHENSION

Summarize

DIRECTIONS Look at the pictures in *Bread, Bread, Bread*. What do you see?

Make notes on the chart.

Summary Notes

Page #	I see . . .
28	
29	
30	

Name _____

WORD WORK

Short a Sound

DIRECTIONS Use letters from the box to make 5 different words.
You can use a letter more than once.

m	t	r	c	f	n

1. b a _____

2.   a n _____

3. r a _____

4.   a _____

5.   a _____

Practice

DIRECTIONS Write a sentence about bread. Use a word with the
short a sound in your sentence. Circle the word.

_____

_____

Name _____

WORD WORK

Adding y Endings

Describing words are called adjectives. Many adjectives have a *y* ending.

DIRECTIONS Make these words adjectives by adding a *y* ending.

stick _____

cloud _____

milk _____

hill _____

dirt _____

Practice

DIRECTIONS Look through *Bread, Bread, Bread*. Find two adjectives that have *y* endings. Write them here.

_____

_____

Name _____

LESSON TEST

Multiple-Choice

DIRECTIONS Write the letter of the best answer for each question on the line.

_____ 1. Which of these is not bread?
- A. pizza
- C. pretzel
- B. bagel
- D. wheat

_____ 2. What can bread do for you?
- A. It makes you sick.
- C. It makes you smart.
- B. It makes you strong.
- D. It makes you silly.

_____ 3. What is another good title for *Bread, Bread, Bread*?
- A. Crunchy Bread
- C. Bread Around the World
- B. Bread for Sale!
- D. Flat and Round Breads

_____ 4. What is an important idea in *Bread, Bread, Bread*?
- A. Bread is popular in the United States.
- B. Bread comes from wheat.
- C. People all over share a love for bread.
- D. Bread is baked.

Short Answer

What do you like to eat on your bread? Write a sentence about it.

_____

_____

Sam's Story

BACKGROUND

"Sam's Story" is a short story from Edward Marshall's modern-day classic, *Three by the Sea*. In this much-loved book, three children—Sam, Lolly, and Spider—have just eaten lunch and are told they must wait a bit before they can go back in swimming. To amuse themselves, they decide to tell their favorite cat and rat stories. Sam's story, about a rat who buys a cat, greatly amuses his audience and helps make the time out of the water pass more quickly.

James Edward Marshall (1942–1992) wrote and illustrated more than 70 books for children, including the award-winning "George and Martha" series. Marshall, who often wrote under the pseudonym of Edward Marshall, illustrated his first children's book—*Plink, Plink, Plink* by Byrd Baylor—in 1971. Although *Plink, Plink, Plink* was not a commercial success, it did solidify in Marshall's own mind a strong desire to draw pictures for children. A year later, Marshall's *George and Martha* was chosen as one of the *New York Times* ten best illustrated children's books for 1972 and as an ALA Notable book.

BIBLIOGRAPHY Students might enjoy listening to a read-aloud of another Edward Marshall story. Here are three favorites, two of which are follow-ups to *Three by the Sea*:

THREE UP A TREE (Lexile 160)   FOX ALL WEEK (Lexile 170)   FOUR ON THE SHORE (Lexile 210)

How to Introduce the Reading

The opening activity for "Sam's Story" (student book page 35) is an anticipation guide similar to the one students completed before reading *Bread, Bread, Bread*. As you'll recall, an anticipation guide is designed to activate prior knowledge and provide students with a clear-cut purpose for reading.

Before they read "Sam's Story," students will consider some commonly held beliefs about animals—for example, *dogs like to chase cats*—and decide whether they're true or false. This activity is an important first step in understanding the subject (a cat and a rat) and the theme (unlikely friends) of Marshall's story.

After students finish their anticipation guides, have volunteers discuss their answers. If possible, ask them to support their true/false decisions with stories from their own lives. Then ask them to speculate: *Can a dog be friends with a cat? Can a cat be friends with a bird? Can a rat be friends with a cat?* If you like, return to students' speculations after they finish the reading.

Other Reading

As a follow-up to "Sam's Story," read aloud another animal book for young readers. Here are three favorites.

(Lexile 40)   (Lexile 80)   (Lexile 100)

STUDENT PAGES 35–48

Skills and Strategies Overview

PREREADING	word web
READING LEVEL	Lexile 60
RESPONSE	draw
VOCABULARY	✦fine ✦shining ✦friend ✦sure ✦favorite
COMPREHENSION	retell
WORD WORK	short *o*
MORE WORD WORK	suffixes *ed, er,* and *ing*
WRITING	two sentences

OTHER RESOURCES

The first **four** pages of this teacher's lesson describe Parts I–IV of the lesson. Also included are these **six** blackline masters. Use them to reinforce key elements of the lesson.

Vocabulary

STUDYING WORDS
Before Reading
DIRECTIONS Connect the word pair with its contraction.

we are	it's
it is	I'm
I am	he'll
he will	we're
she is	that's
they are	she's
that is	they're

Practice
DIRECTIONS Write a sentence about cats. Use one contraction.

Prereading

BEFORE YOU READ
Listening Guide
DIRECTIONS Listen to the story.
Each time your teacher stops, answer one of these questions.

page 39 What does the rat see on his walk?

page 40 What does the rat buy with his dime?

page 42 What question does the rat ask the cat?

page 43 Why do you think the cat wants to be alone with the rat?

page 45 What is funny about the end of the story?

Comprehension

COMPREHENSION
Story String
DIRECTIONS Use this Story String to tell what happens in "Sam's Story."

First,

Then,

After that,

At the end,

Word Work

WORD WORK
Short o Sound
DIRECTIONS Complete each word using the vowel *o*. Write the vowel on the line.

1. p _ nd
2. s _ ft
3. m _ b
4. l _ t
5. cl _ ck

Practice
DIRECTIONS Write 3 words from the list that have the same short *o* sound you hear in *pop*.

| sand | mom | tap | top | sob |

6.
7.
8.

More Word Work

MORE WORD WORK
Suffixes with ed, er, and ing
DIRECTIONS Add the suffix *ed, er,* or *ing* to each word below to make a new word.

1. keep + ing
2. own + er
3. warm + er
4. walk + ed
5. pick + ing

Practice
DIRECTIONS Look at "Sam's Story" again. Answer this question. What word in the story has an *ing* ending?

Assessment

LESSON TEST
Multiple-Choice
DIRECTIONS Write the letter of the best answer for each question on the line.

____ 1. Why does the rat buy the cat?
A. The rat wants cheese.   C. The man tells him to.
B. The rat wants a friend.   D. The cat has no home.

____ 2. Where does the rat take the cat?
A. to a house   C. to the city
B. to a farm   D. to the beach

____ 3. What is the cat's favorite food?
A. rat   C. fish
B. cheese   D. cat food

____ 4. What is an important idea in "Sam's Story"?
A. Pets can make you feel good.
B. Anyone can be a friend.
C. Cheese is good for all animals.
D. Cats and rats usually get along.

Short Answer
Tell what you like about the rat. Then tell what you like about the cat.

BEFORE YOU READ

Read aloud the directions at the top of student book page 36. Explain that students are about to read a short story about a cat and a rat. Then have the class write on the word web three or more words that they associate with cats. When they finish, discuss their webs. Make a class list of cat characteristics on the board. If you have time, direct students to complete another web, this time for the word *rat*.

Motivation Strategy

CONNECTING WITH STUDENTS
Ask students to tell a personal story about a time they witnessed two animals interacting. Have them explain which animals were there and what they were doing. Did the animals fight or get along? Ask: *Has anyone seen two animals that you never thought could be friends get along well? What about a dog and a cat or a cat and a mouse?*

Studying Words

CONTEXT CLUES
Use the Studying Words activity on student book page 37 as a way of introducing contractions to students, or reinforcing what they've learned in a previous lesson. Ask students to read along with you as you work your way through the four sample contractions at the top of the page. Then have them complete the cross-out activity in the center of the page. Be sure students eliminate *do not, would not,* and *she will.* Finish the lesson by having students form their own contractions for *he is, she will,* and *we have.*

After you finish page 37, you might offer a brief introduction to vocabulary words in "Sam's Story." Choose several that you think will be challenging for students and have them discuss. Then ask students to explain what they should do if they come to an unfamiliar word in a story. Remind them of the value of searching for **context clues** by finding the following vocabulary words in the story: *fine, shining, friend, sure,* and *favorite.* Explain how the sentences around each word can help them find meaning.

Prereading Strategies

WORD WEB
The prereading **word web** on student book page 36 serves two important purposes. First, it will prompt students to do some initial thinking about cats and what they are like. This in turn will help them better understand the irony of a cat choosing cheese rather than a rodent for his favorite meal. Second, the word web will encourage students to make one or more personal connections to the text, since it asks students to write about what *they* know about cats.

READ ALOUD
Although it might at first seem "babyish" to listen while a story is read aloud, students will soon learn that listening as someone else reads can make the plot, characters, and key ideas easier to understand—and enjoy. Encourage students to follow along in the book as they listen. This way, they can mark passages that they think are important or confusing. After listening to the first page of the story (student book page 38), have students pause and reflect on what they've heard thus far. Ask one or more guided reading questions to determine their level of comprehension. Or, ask them to complete the first part of the listening guide blackline master on page 101. When you've finished checking students' responses to page 38, move on to page 39. Once again, read the page aloud and assess students' comprehension. Read on to the bottom of the second page. There, you'll want to pause again and check comprehension. Continue this read-pause-check pattern the whole way through the story.

To support your read aloud, use the **Before You Read** blackline master on page 101.

MY PURPOSE
Read aloud the purpose statement on student book page 36, and then ask a volunteer to retell the class's purpose for reading. Encourage students to jot down in the "My Notes" section details that relate to this purpose.

II. READ

Response Strategy

FIRST READING   Keep in mind the value of having readers **pause and reflect** at several different points during the reading. You'll find that students get so much more from a text if they jot down their ideas as they go, rather than wait until they've finished.

Comprehension Strategy

SECOND READING   **Stopping and retelling** the action of a story can help readers clarify in their own minds what they've learned. Because "Sam's Story" is a longer selection, you'll want to provide at least two opportunities for students to pause, reflect, and **retell.** Explain the process by directing students' attention to the first Stop and Retell box on page 41. Discuss the kinds of notes a reader might make at this point in the story. Then have students complete the Stop and Retell boxes on student pages 43 and 45.

For more help with **Comprehension,** assign the blackline master on page 102.

Discussion Questions

COMPREHENSION   1. Who are the main characters in "Sam's Story"? *(the cat and the rat)*

2. What does the rat buy at the store? *(a cat)*

3. What question does the rat want the cat to answer? *(The rat wants to know what the cat most likes to eat.)*

4. What happens when the rat and cat are alone? *(The cat tells the rat his favorite food is cheese.)*

CRITICAL THINKING   5. Why do you think the rat wants a cat? *(Answers will vary. Possible: He wants a friend, and he thinks the cat will make a good one.)*

6. How do cats and rats usually get along? *(Possible: Usually, cats chase rats and try to kill and even eat them.)*

7. What's funny about the end of this story? *(Possible: It seems like the cat might want to eat the rat because he wants to be alone with the rat. But, he doesn't eat the rat. Instead, he tells the rat he likes cheese best.)*

Reread

THIRD READING   If students have trouble answering the above comprehension and critical thinking questions, or if they have a hard time retelling the key events of the story, you might encourage them to do a third reading. Divide the class into small groups. Have group members take turns reading the story aloud. When groups have finished, ask them to discuss the story. Invite them to think about the character of the rat and figure out why he acts the way he does.

Word Work

SHORT O   The Word Work lesson on student book page 46 offers students some review work with the **short *o*** sound in one-syllable words. Begin by reading aloud the directions at the top of the page. Then have students complete their list of three short *o* words and discuss their choices. Break the words apart sound by sound. Then have students write a sentence in which one or more short *o* words appear.

For additional practice, see the **Word Work** blackline master on page 103.

More Word Work

SUFFIXES ED, ER, ING The Word Work lesson on student book page 47 presents a lesson on the **suffixes *ed, er,* and *ing.*** Begin by asking a volunteer to read aloud the explanation at the top of the page. Help students understand how a word changes meaning when a suffix is added. Next, work through the examples for the three different suffixes. Ask students to suggest additional words with the same suffixes. Then have them work in groups to complete the activity at the bottom of the page.

Assign the **More Word Work** blackline master on page 104 if you feel students need more practice with *ed, er,* and *ing* endings.

III. WRITE

BRAINSTORM The prewriting activity at the top of student book page 48 asks students to think of words that describe the cat and the rat. To make the activity more interesting, try dividing the class into two groups. Have groups work together to brainstorm a list of either cat or rat adjectives. If students seem stuck, remind them that an important part of reading a story is understanding how the characters act, feel about themselves, and feel about others. Explain that you can tell a lot about the character of the rat just by the fact that he is so interested in hearing what the cat likes to eat. Ask: *What does this tell you about the rat? Is he kind or mean? Is he thoughtful or thoughtless?* Then come together a class and read both groups' lists aloud.

WRITE TWO SENTENCES Have students keep their list of adjectives in front of them as they write their **two sentences** about the cat and rat. To get them started, have students read down their lists once more and highlight the two words they think best describe the animals. Then ask them to write a draft of their sentences using the dictionary as needed for spelling questions. When they've finished, ask students to exchange papers. Post the following Writing Rubric on the board and ask students to assess their partners' sentences.

WRITING RUBRIC Have students use this rubric when assessing their partners' writing.

Do both of the sentences

- begin with a capital letter and end with an end mark?
- tell about the rat and the cat?
- state a complete thought?

Grammar, Usage, and Mechanics

Create a Writer's Checklist on the board to which students can refer as they edit their work. Checklist items include:

✔ My sentences tell about the cat and the rat.

✔ My sentences begin with a capital letter.

✔ My sentences end with a punctuation mark.

✔ My sentences tell a complete thought.

IV. LOOK BACK

Ask students to think about the ending of the story. What surprised them? Then discuss their overall enjoyment of the reading. Explain that a surprise ending to a story can make a reader want to go back and read the work once more.

To test students' comprehension, use the **Lesson Test** blackline master on page 105.

Name _____

STUDYING WORDS

Before Reading

DIRECTIONS Connect the word pair with its contraction.

we are	it's
it is	I'm
I am	he'll
he will	we're
she is	that's
they are	she's
that is	they're

Practice

DIRECTIONS Write a sentence about cats. Use one contraction.

_____

_____

Name _____

BEFORE YOU READ

Listening Guide

DIRECTIONS Listen to the story.

Each time your teacher stops, answer one of these questions.

page 39   What does the rat see on his walk?

_____

_____

page 40   What does the rat buy with his dime?

_____

_____

page 42   What question does the rat ask the cat?

_____

_____

page 43   Why do you think the cat wants to be alone with the rat?

_____

_____

page 45   What is funny about the end of the story?

_____

_____

Name _____

COMPREHENSION

Story String

DIRECTIONS Use this Story String to tell what happens in "Sam's Story."

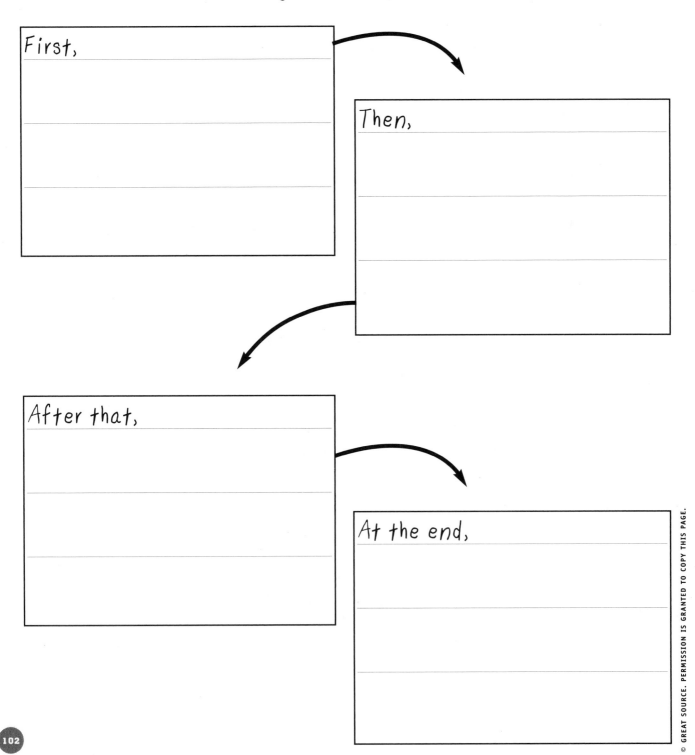

First,

Then,

After that,

At the end,

Name _____

WORD WORK

Short o Sound

DIRECTIONS Complete each word using the vowel *o*. Write the vowel on the line.

1. p   nd

2. s   ft

3. m   b

4. l   t

5. cl   ck

Practice

DIRECTIONS Write 3 words from the list that have the same short *o* sound you hear in *pop*.

> sand   mom   tap   top   sob

6. _____

7. _____

8. _____

Name _____

MORE WORD WORK

Suffixes with
ed, er, and ing

DIRECTIONS Add the suffix *ed*, *er*, or *ing* to each word below to make a new word.

1. keep + ing _____

2. own + er _____

3. warm + er _____

4. walk + ed _____

5. pick + ing _____

Practice

DIRECTIONS Look at "Sam's Story" again. Answer this question.

What word in the story has an *ing* ending?

_____

_____

Name _____

LESSON TEST

Multiple-Choice

DIRECTIONS Write the letter of the best answer for each question on the line.

_____ 1. Why does the rat buy the cat?
    A. The rat wants cheese.   C. The man tells him to.
    B. The rat wants a friend.   D. The cat has no home.

_____ 2. Where does the rat take the cat?
    A. to a house   C. to the city
    B. to a farm   D. to the beach

_____ 3. What is the cat's favorite food?
    A. rat   C. fish
    B. cheese   D. cat food

_____ 4. What is an important idea in "Sam's Story"?
    A. Pets can make you feel good.
    B. Anyone can be a friend.
    C. Cheese is good for all animals.
    D. Cats and rats usually get along.

Short Answer

Tell what you like about the rat. Then tell what you like about the cat.

_____

_____

Shoes, Shoes, Shoes

BACKGROUND

In *Shoes, Shoes, Shoes* (a follow-up to *Bread, Bread, Bread),* children's book author Ann Morris explores in further detail her theme that people of the world have so much in common. Here Morris discusses shoes of the world and the universality of their purpose the world over. From her book, students can learn the universal truth that no matter who they are or where they live, people wear shoes for comfort, protection, and sometimes even for style.

In the text, Morris shows readers different kinds of shoes and explains where they are most popular. In the book's index, she offers additional information on such shoes as leather moccasins (Canada), wooden shoes (Netherlands), wooden sole thongs (Japan), wooden sabots (Spain), and thick-soled sandals (Kenya).

Ann Morris, author, editor, and former teacher, has written several books for children, many of which deal with multicultural themes. An excerpt from her popular *Bread, Bread, Bread,* appears on pages 28–31 of the **Sourcebook**.

BIBLIOGRAPHY Students might enjoy reading another book by Ann Morris. Suggest they look for one of these three at the library:

(Lexile 30)   (Lexile Beginning Reading)   (Not Rated)

How to Introduce the Reading

As their first prereading activity, ask students to complete the web for *shoes* on page 49. A web such as this will provide a strong introduction to the subject of the selection, as well as act as a starting point for the kinds of active reader connections students need to make to get the most out of the text.

Begin by reading aloud the prompt at the top of the page. Brainstorm with students some of the different kinds of shoes they might list on the web. Have them look around the room to see what types they see. Ask: *Who is wearing sneakers? Who is wearing shoes with no laces? Who is wearing dress-up shoes?* Segue from there into a discussion of what shoes can reveal about a person's occupation, likes and dislikes, personality, and so on.

Other Reading

Continue your exploration of communities around the world by asking students to read one of the following books:

(Lexile 90)	(Lexile 90)	(Lexile not rated)

Shoes, Shoes, Shoes

Skills and Strategies Overview

PREREADING	preview
READING LEVEL	Lexile 100
RESPONSE	question
VOCABULARY	✧ice ✧school ✧dancing ✧walking ✧riding
COMPREHENSION	visualize
WORD WORK	short vowels
MORE WORD WORK	adding *s*
WRITING	3 sentences

OTHER RESOURCES

The first **four** pages of this teacher's lesson describe Parts I–IV of the lesson. Also included are these **six** blackline masters. Use them to reinforce key elements of the lesson.

Vocabulary

Prereading

Comprehension

Word Work

More Word Work

Assessment

BEFORE YOU READ

Discuss **previewing** with students. Explain that the purpose of a preview is to give readers a kind of "heads up" about the subject and important ideas in the reading. Then have students look at the Preview Checklist on student book page 50. Discuss each item on the list and why it's important. Finish by directing students to preview *Shoes, Shoes, Shoes.* Ask them to make a few notes about what they saw in their reading journals.

Motivation Strategy

MOTIVATING STUDENTS Have volunteers tell about a favorite pair of shoes, or invite all students to wear their favorite pair on the day you begin the unit. Have students spend a few minutes quickwriting a description of their shoes. Then, come together as a group and discuss. Ask students to explain where they got their shoes and why they like them. Make a list of adjectives students use when describing their shoes. Keep the list posted on the board and ask students to review it before they complete the writing assignment at the end of the unit.

Studying Words

CONTEXT CLUES Use the Studying Words activity on student book page 51 to strengthen students' understanding of **s plurals**. Read aloud the directions at the top of the page, and then have students read the plurals in the box. If students are comfortable making plurals with the letter *s*, ask them to complete the activity on the bottom of the page on their own.

To begin, show students key vocabulary words in "Shoes, Shoes, Shoes": *ice, school, dancing, walking,* and *riding.* Review how to use **context clues** to find the definition of an unfamiliar word. Remind the class that good readers look for context clues in surrounding sentences and in the illustrations. Direct students' attention to page 54. What might they do if they didn't know the definitions for the words *school* and *dancing*?

Prereading Strategies

PREVIEW The directions at the top of student book page 50 explain how and why readers **preview** a text before they begin reading. Explain to students that it's a good idea to make a note of the questions and comments that occur to them while they're previewing. Help students set up a preview chart in their reading journals that corresponds with the Preview Checklist. Or, use the **Before You Read** blackline master on page 113 to support the activity.

QUICKWRITE As an additional prereading activity, have students do a one-minute **quickwrite** on the topic of shoes. Encourage students to write continuously during the preview—without lifting their pencils from the page, if possible. Keep in mind that quickwriting is an effective prereading strategy because it activates prior knowledge and helps students make a strong connection to the subject of the work.

MY PURPOSE Read the purpose statement on page 50 aloud: *What are shoes for? How many kinds of shoes are there?* Help students understand that their purpose for reading will be to find answers to these two questions. Because this may be students' first exposure to a multi-part purpose, you might want to make a "permanent record" of both purposes on the board and remind students what they're looking for several different points in the reading.

II. READ

Response Strategy

FIRST READING Before students begin their first readings, explain the response strategy of asking during-reading **questions.** Point out the example in the "My Notes" area of student book page 52. Explain that this question—*Where can you find shoes?*—is an example of one that might occur to students as they read the information on the page. Remind students that keeping track of their questions as they go is far easier than trying to generate a list of questions after the reading. In addition, it can help them more effectively process the key ideas in a work.

Comprehension Strategy

SECOND READING Be sure students understand that you'd like them to **visualize**, or make mental pictures of, the shoes Morris describes in her book. Like asking questions, visualizing can help readers process what they've read. It also can encourage the reader to make meaningful connections to a text.

For more help with **Comprehension,** assign the blackline master on page 114.

Discussion Questions

COMPREHENSION 1. Who is the author of *Shoes, Shoes, Shoes*? (Ann Morris)

2. What does it mean that shoes "come in twos"? *(They come in pairs.)*

CRITICAL THINKING 3. What would you say is Morris's most important point about shoes? *(Everybody needs shoes.)*

4. What are some reasons people wear shoes? *(Possible: for protection, fashion, comfort)*

5. What are your favorite shoes and why? *(Answers will vary. Encourage students to offer a full description of their favorite pair.)*

6. How can you tell that *Shoes, Shoes, Shoes* is a nonfiction book? *(It tells about something that is real instead of imaginary.)*

Reread

THIRD READING As you know, rereading a selection for a second (or third) time can greatly increase comprehension. Tell students that when they reread Morris's text, they should watch for specific information on types of shoes and who wears them. Ask, *What shoes does a dancer wear? What about a construction worker or an athlete?* Have students make notes in the margins of their books.

Word Work

SHORT VOWELS The Word Work lesson on student book page 56 offers students some review work on **short vowel sounds.** Begin by asking students to name and pronounce five short vowel sounds: /a/ as in *cap,* /e/ as in *pen,* /i/ as in *inch,* /o/ as in *stop,* and /u/ as in *tug.* Review each of these words sound by sound. Then write the vowel sounds on the board and have students work in groups to brainstorm a list of five or more words per sound. Then have students work on their own to complete the activity on page 56. When they finish, discuss their efforts.

For additional practice, see the **Word Work** blackline master on page 115.

More Word Work

PLURALS WITH S Use the second Word Work lesson on student book page 57 to offer students additional practice in making **plurals with s**. Before you begin, review the work students did with *s* and *es* plurals after reading *Mice Squeak, We Speak*. Ask, *How do you know if you're supposed to use an s or an es to form a plural?* Then read aloud the text at the top of page 57. Model how to make plural the following words: *shirt, skirt, shoe,* and *pant*. Tell students that adding *s* results in two sounds—/s/, as in *lips*, and /z/, as in *mugs*. Then assign the activity.

Assign the **Word Work** blackline master on page 116 for more practice forming plurals.

III. WRITE

BRAINSTORM Use the drawing activity at the top of student book page 58 as a prewriting exercise. Invite students to use as much detail as they can as they **draw** their wardrobe items. When they finish, invite them to share what they've drawn. Note on the board adjectives students use in their descriptions. Then work together as a class to brainstorm additional adjectives that can be used to describe the shoes they wear. Keep the list on the board and encourage students to refer to it as they write.

WRITE THREE SENTENCES After you finish brainstorming, assign the bottom half of the Draw and Write page (student book page 58). Read the directions aloud to students and be sure they understand that their assignment is to write **three sentences** that describe the items they drew. Finish your instructions by reminding students of the characteristics of a sentence. Ask them to keep in mind the following: A sentence is a group of words that states a complete thought. A sentence begins with a capital letter and ends with a punctuation mark.

After students finish writing, have them reread their work to be sure they've included several descriptive words in their sentences.

WRITING RUBRIC Use this rubric to help with a quick assessment of students' writing.

Do students' sentences

- begin with a capital letter and end with a punctuation mark?

- express a complete thought?

- include adjectives that describe the shoes they drew?

Grammar, Usage, and Mechanics

Create a Writer's Checklist on the board to which students can refer as they edit their work. Checklist items include:

✔ My sentence begins with a capital letter and ends with a punctuation mark.

✔ My sentence tells a complete thought.

✔ My sentence contains descriptive words.

IV. LOOK BACK

Reflect with students on their responses to *Shoes, Shoes, Shoes*. Were they able to read it with ease? Why or why not? Discuss actions a reader might take if a selection appears challenging. These include rereading, taking additional notes, and skimming for key details.

To test students' comprehension, use the **Lesson Test** blackline master on page 117.

Name _____

STUDYING WORDS

Before Reading

DIRECTIONS Read the words in the box.

Then choose the word that goes with each clue.

> walking   riding   dancing   school   ice

1. Place where you learn _____

2. Something a ballerina is doing _____

3. Horses are for _____

4. The opposite of <u>running</u> _____

5. Used to make a drink cold _____

Practice

Write a question that uses one of the words in the box. Then write an answer.

_____

_____

Name _____

BEFORE YOU READ

Preview

DIRECTIONS Use the Preview Checklist on page 50 to help you preview *Shoes, Shoes, Shoes*.

Write your notes on this chart.

What the title tells me . . .	What the first sentence tells me . . .
What the photos tell me . . .	**What the last sentence tells me . . .**

Then write a prediction about the story.

My prediction: _____

_____

Name _____

COMPREHENSION

Directed Reading

DIRECTIONS Work with a reading partner. Answer these questions. Look at *Shoes, Shoes, Shoes* whenever you need to.

1. Why do shoes come in twos?

_____

2. What are some different types of shoes?

_____

3. Where can you find shoes?

_____

4. What is one reason you wear shoes?

_____

5. What is another reason?

_____

Name _____

WORD WORK

Short Vowels

DIRECTIONS Use a vowel from the box to best complete the words below. Write the word in the right column.

> a   e   i   o   u

1. We can make a st___ck of pancakes.   st___ck

2. She wore r___d shoes.   r___d

3. A r___g goes on the floor.   r___g

4. Who will s___t near me?   s___t

5. She put the gift in the b___x.   b___x

Practice

DIRECTIONS Write 2 words from the box with short vowel sounds.

> go   pin   tag   sky   pie

6. _____

7. _____

Name _____

MORE WORD WORK

Adding s

DIRECTIONS Read the words in the word box.

Make each word plural by adding an *s*.

Word Box

| bat | team | lip | pan | mug |

1. _____

2. _____

3. _____

4. _____

5. _____

Practice

DIRECTIONS Find two plural words in *Shoes, Shoes, Shoes*. Write them here.

6. _____   7. _____

Name _____

LESSON TEST

Multiple-Choice

DIRECTIONS Write the letter of the best answer for each question on the line.

_____ 1. Ann Morris says shoes come in _____.
A. a set   C. bags
B. twos   D. boxes

_____ 2. Shoes are not for _____.
A. dancing   C. playing
B. riding   D. sleeping

_____ 3. People wear shoes for _____.
A. work   C. play
B. protection   D. all of these reasons

_____ 4. What is an important idea in *Shoes, Shoes, Shoes*?
A. Everywhere you go, people wear shoes.
B. Old shoes are best.
C. Everyone needs lots of shoes.
D. It's fun to go barefoot.

Short Answer

Write about the best shoes you ever had. You may use the back of this page.

_____

_____

Building a House

BACKGROUND

Byron Barton is the author and illustrator of dozens of well-received books for children, including *Airport, Dinosaurs, The Three Bears,* and *Machines at Work.* His *I Want to Be an Astronaut* is a perennial favorite of young readers, as is his version of *Little Red Hen.* In addition to drawing his own work, Barton also has illustrated for other well-known authors, including Constance C. Greene, Sid Hoff, and Marjorie Weinman Sharmat.

On **Sourcebook** pages 62–67, you'll find a reprint of Barton's *Building a House.* Here, Barton presents step-by-step the process of building a house from the ground up. Barton's use of simple yet vibrant language makes for accessible—but never simplistic—reading. Notice how his charming and colorful art brings to life the complicated procedure of preparing a site, pouring the foundation, and framing the structure. Likewise, his explanation of how the house gets its "guts"—electricity, plumbing, and so on—is simple enough that even your most unsophisticated readers will have no trouble discovering meaning.

Because the subject of Barton's book is construction, you might want to use it to create a link between your reading and science or art curricula. Invite students to reflect upon the process of construction of a building. Then have students draw pictures of their dream house. Have students write a description of what they built.

BIBLIOGRAPHY Try creating a classroom library of Byron Barton books. Be sure to include the following three titles:

(Lexile Beginning Reading)   (Lexile 100)   (Lexile 290)

How to Introduce the Reading

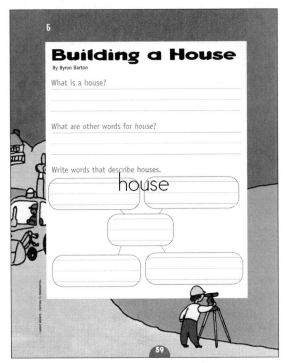

Begin by asking students how many have seen a building being built. See if they can name steps in the process, which may include: digging a basement; pouring the foundation; laying the subfloor; framing the walls; building the roof; adding bricks, stones, or stucco; and completing the plumbing and electrical work.

Then explain to students that they will be reading a nonfiction book that describes how a house is built. Ask them to think about the word *home* and what it means to them. Invite volunteers to describe different types of homes. Then direct students' attention to student book page 59. Read aloud the questions on the page and point out the web. Ask students to write their ideas on the lines, or use the page to help you conduct a whole-class warm-up activity.

Other Reading

After students finish their webs, suggest they browse through a couple of books that relate to the information discussed in *Building a House*. The following would work well.

(Lexile 570)   (Lexile N/A)   (Lexile N/A)

Building a House

Skills and Strategies Overview

PREREADING	predict and preview
READING LEVEL	Lexile 100
RESPONSE	mark
VOCABULARY	✦bricklayer ✦fireplace ✦plumber ✦electrician ✦carpenter
COMPREHENSION	retell
WORD WORK	short *i*
MORE WORD WORK	compound words
WRITING	3 sentences

OTHER RESOURCES

The first **four** pages of this teacher's lesson describe Parts I–IV of the lesson. Also included are these **six** blackline masters. Use them to reinforce key elements of the lesson.

Vocabulary

Prereading

Comprehension

Word Work

More Word Work

Assessment

I. BEFORE YOU READ

Discuss the work students did on student book page 59. List on the board the words students associate with *house*. Keep the list on the board for the remainder of the unit so that students can consult it as needed during the reading and to help them complete the writing assignment. Then, direct students' attention to page 60. Read aloud the information under Before You Read. Discuss the importance of making predictions and how a reader's predictions can help him or her get more from a text. Then assign the activity.

Motivation Strategies

MOTIVATING STUDENTS Have students draw a picture of their own home or a house they admire. If you like, show them how to make a sketch of the house that indicates room divisions. Then have students design their own. Encourage students to use color to add vibrancy to their pictures. Ask, *Which colors could you use to make a house look warm and inviting?*

CONNECTING WITH STUDENTS Ask students to tell a personal story about moving into a new home or helping someone move into a new house. Ask them to tell the incident in chronological order as a way of offering more practice with this type of organization. Later, you might have them write journal entries on the same topic.

Studying Words

CONTEXT CLUES Use the Studying Words on student book page 61 as a way to troubleshoot vocabulary problems. After working through the page, you might decide to teach a short vocabulary lesson on using **context clues.**

The ability to use context clues can greatly improve students' reading fluency and comprehension. Help students use context clues to determine the meaning of some of the more challenging words in *Building a House,* including: *bricklayer, fireplace, plumber, electrician,* and *carpenter.*

To begin, model using context clues by saying: *I see the word* plumber, *but I'm not sure what it means. I'll reread the sentence in which it appears. I'll pay close attention to the words around it that I do know. I know the sentence tells about putting in water pipes, so I can assume that a plumber is someone who installs pipes for water.*

Invite volunteers to try using context clues for other vocabulary words. Then have students complete the **Studying Words** blackline master on page 124.

Prereading Strategies

PREVIEW AND PREDICT As a prereading activity, students are asked to **preview** the Byron Barton selection and then **predict** what they think they'll learn about building a house. As you know, making predictions about a text can activate students' interest while at the same time give them a purpose for reading. In this case, they'll read to find out if they did in fact learn everything they set out to learn.

THINK-PAIR-SHARE As an additional prereading activity, have students work together on a **think-pair-and-share** that explores their knowledge of the kinds of people needed to build a house. Have them begin by marking "agree" or "disagree" in response to four statements that relate to the selection. Then ask them to share their answers with a partner. They'll finish by naming people who work on a house site.

Use the **Before You Read** blackline master on page 125 to support this activity.

MY PURPOSE Read aloud the purpose statement on page 60. Be sure students understand that you'd like them to think about the people who make a house and what they do to complete the project. Students should keep this purpose in mind as they are reading.

II. READ

Response Strategy

FIRST READING Before students begin *Building a House,* explain the various ways readers **mark** a text while reading. Tell the class that they might use a highlighter to set off words they think are important or puzzling or to isolate important ideas. Marking a text also means writing their questions and comments in the margins of the selection. This will slow readers down, which in turn can help them more effectively process what they've read. Make sure students understand not to mark library books.

Comprehension Strategy

SECOND READING Be sure students understand that as they read the Barton selection, they'll need to stop to **retell** what they've learned. Retelling is a good strategy to use with longer or more challenging texts since it forces students to reflect on important information as they go, instead of waiting until the end to gather facts and details. Later, students can use their interrupter notes to help them complete the **Comprehension** blackline master on page 126.

Discussion Questions

COMPREHENSION
1. Who is the author of *Building a House*? *(Byron Barton)*

2. Is the book fiction or nonfiction? How do you know? *(It's nonfiction. You can tell because it gives real, not imaginary information.)*

3. What does a carpenter do? *(A carpenter makes the frame for the foundation of the house, builds the floor and walls, and adds the roof. Carpenters also put in windows and doors.)*

4. What does a bricklayer do? *(A bricklayer lays bricks for the frame of the house. He builds a fireplace and the chimney as well.)*

CRITICAL THINKING
5. What would you say is the hardest part of building a house? *(Possible: I think building the roof is probably the hardest. You're so high up when you're working on a roof, I'd be scared I'd fall.)*

6. How is the job of a plumber different from the job of a carpenter? How is it the same? *(Possible: It's different because a plumber works with pipes for water and an electrician works with wires for lights. It's the same because both jobs are done inside the house, after it is pretty much built.)*

Reread

THIRD READING If you feel students need additional help with the selection, ask them to reread again, this time with an eye to the sequence of events the author describes. Give them a sequence organizer. Then have them make notes on the organizer about the process of building a house. Remind students not to worry about writing full sentences while reading. It's much more important that they get the information down in any form and return to it later if they want to polish things up.

Word Work

SHORT I The Word Work lesson on student book page 68 offers students some practice with the **short *i*** vowel sound. Begin the lesson by brainstorming with the class a list of short *i* words. Then write a list of short and long *i* words on the board for students to sort (*bit, bite; fit, fight; mitt, might*). When the class has finished, assign the activities on page 68. Then follow up with the **Word Work** blackline master on page 127.

More Word Work

COMPOUND WORDS The Word Work lesson on student page 69 offers an introduction to **compound words**. Have students complete the exercise on page 69 and then brainstorm a list of compound words on their own.

To make the activity more challenging, have them think of compound words that relate somehow to the selection. (Ideas might include *bricklayer, fireplace,* and *inside,* as well as all compound words that relate to construction.) If necessary, have students explain the relationship.

Assign the **More Word Work** blackline master on page 128 if you feel students need practice writing compound words.

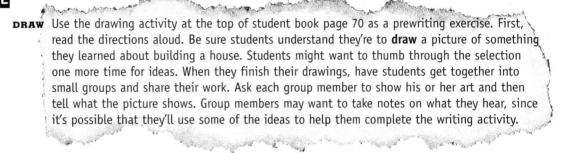

III. WRITE

DRAW Use the drawing activity at the top of student book page 70 as a prewriting exercise. First, read the directions aloud. Be sure students understand they're to **draw** a picture of something they learned about building a house. Students might want to thumb through the selection one more time for ideas. When they finish their drawings, have students get together into small groups and share their work. Ask each group member to show his or her art and then tell what the picture shows. Group members may want to take notes on what they hear, since it's possible that they'll use some of the ideas to help them complete the writing activity.

WRITE YOUR SENTENCES After students complete their group work, assign the bottom half of the Draw and Write page (page 70). Read the directions aloud to students and be sure they understand that their assignment is to write **three sentences** that tell about what they drew. These sentences should also explain what they learned from reading the Barton selection. Finish your instructions by brainstorming the characteristics of a sentence. Remind the class that a sentence is a group of words that states a complete thought. A sentence begins with a capital letter and ends with a punctuation mark.

After students finish writing, have them reread their work to be sure they've written at least three sentences about building a house.

WRITING RUBRIC Use this rubric to help with a quick assessment of students' writing.

Do students' sentences

- begin with a capital letter and end with a punctuation mark?

- express a complete thought?

- stay focused on the subject of building a house?

Grammar, Usage, and Mechanics

Create a Writer's Checklist on the board to which students can refer as they edit their work. Checklist items include:

√ I have written four or more sentences.

√ Every sentence is about my drawing and what I learned from reading *Building a House.*

√ My sentences all begin with a capital letter.

√ My sentences all end with a punctuation mark.

IV. LOOK BACK

Finish the lesson by asking students to comment on their enjoyment of *Building a House.* Would they be interested in learning more about construction? Why or why not? Where might they go to find additional information on this subject?

To test students' comprehension, use the **Lesson Test** blackline master on page 129.

Name _____

STUDYING WORDS

Before Reading

DIRECTIONS Read each sentence. Then write what you think the underlined word means.

1. A <u>bricklayer</u> built a wall outside our apartment building.

I think bricklayer means _____ .

2. A <u>carpenter</u> made a wood frame for the wall.

I think carpenter means _____ .

3. A <u>plumber</u> came to fix the old fountain in the courtyard.

I think plumber means _____ .

4. The <u>electrician</u> said he could add lights to the wall.

I think electrician means _____ .

Practice

Use *fireplace* in a sentence about a house.
Give clues about what *fireplace* means.

_____

Name _____

BEFORE YOU READ

Think-Pair-and-Share

DIRECTIONS Read the statements about building a house.

If you agree, check the YES box. If you disagree, check the NO box.

Share your ideas with a reading partner.

YES	NO

 The first thing to do in building a house is put up the walls.

 A plumber lays wire for lights.

 It takes a lot of people to build a house.

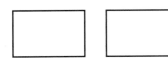 Wood is used to frame the house.

Write

DIRECTIONS On the lines below, list some of the people who help build a house.

_____

_____

Name _____

COMPREHENSION

Reciprocal Reading

DIRECTIONS Get together with a reading partner. Discuss these questions together. Then write answers on the lines. Check your book if you need to.

1. What is the first step in building a house?

_____

_____

2. Name one step that happens next.

_____

_____

3. What is the last step?

_____

_____

4. What do you think is the main idea of *Building a House*?

_____

Name _____

WORD WORK

Short i Sound

DIRECTIONS Read the words in the word box.

Write the words that have the short *i* sound on the lines below.

| find   slip   miss   kite   drip   sign   size   lip   little |

Words with Short i Sound

1. _____   4. _____

2. _____   5. _____

3. _____

6. Can you name the vowel sound the other words make? _____

Practice

DIRECTIONS Choose one of the words you listed on the lines.

Use it in a sentence.

_____

_____

_____

Name _____

MORE WORD WORK

Compound Words

You can make a compound word by joining two small words. For example:

score + card = scorecard

DIRECTIONS Join these small words together to form compound words. Write the words on the lines. One has been done for you.

1. book + keeper = bookkeeper

2. short + stop =

3. in + side =

Practice

DIRECTIONS Here are two lines of small words. Make compound words by connecting a word in List A to a word in List B. An example has been done for you.

List A	List B
1. step	mother
2. grand	place
3. mail	sister
4. fire	box

Name _____

LESSON TEST

Multiple-Choice

DIRECTIONS Write the letter of the best answer for each question on the line.

_____ 1. What type of book is *Building a House*?

    A. nonfiction   C. poetry

    B. fiction   D. play

_____ 2. Which of the following is NOT a job for a carpenter?

    A. putting in windows C. building walls
    and doors

    B. making the roof   D. laying bricks

_____ 3. Who makes the fireplace in a house?

    A. the carpenter   C. the plumber

    B. the bricklayer   D. the electrician

_____ 4. What is the main idea in *Building a House*?

    A. You're lucky if you have a nice house.

    B. Carpenters have terrible jobs.

    C. It takes a lot of people and talent to build a house.

    D. Bulldozers make building a house easier.

Short Answer

Imagine you were going to help build a house. What job would you most like to do? Why?

_____

_____

Water

BACKGROUND

Though he is most known for his Moonbear picture books, Vermont author Frank Asch has written in other categories of children's literature, as evidenced in this nonfiction piece.

In simple, yet vividly descriptive prose, Asch brings water to life. With short, declarative sentences, the author runs through a litany of definitions, from the specific ("Water is rain. Water is dew.") to the abstract ("Water is high in the sky. Water is deep in the earth."). Readers come away with a deeper appreciation of this often-overlooked resource.

BIBLIOGRAPHY Students might enjoy reading other books by Frank Asch. *The Earth and I*, with a Lexile level of 50, is perfect for the struggling reader. Both *Moonbear's Dream* (Lexile 290) and *Song of the North* (Lexile 340) are beyond the Lexile level of *Water* (Lexile 140), but their high interest and helpful illustrations make them wonderful additions to your classroom library and great read-alouds.

(Lexile 340)   (Lexile 50)   (Lexile 290)

How to Introduce the Reading

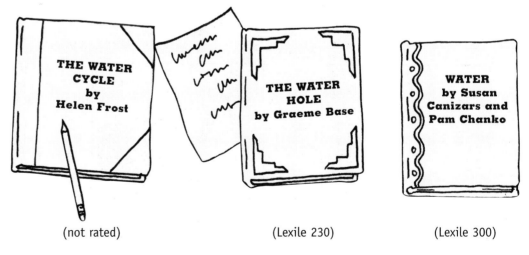

Introduce the selection by working with students to fill in the web for water on page 71. Talk about places where they can find water. List their ideas on the board. Then have students choose four places to list on their individual webs.

The web is designed not only to get students thinking about water in general but also to narrow their thoughts away from the broad topic of water to the more specific topic (where water can be found) related to the selection.

Other Reading

Read aloud these other high-interest nonfiction books. Use them as valuable cross-curricular links to a science unit on water:

THE WATER CYCLE by Helen Frost

THE WATER HOLE by Graeme Base

WATER by Susan Canizars and Pam Chanko

(not rated)   (Lexile 230)   (Lexile 300)

Water

STUDENT PAGES 71–80

Skills and Strategies Overview

PREREADING	anticipation guide
READING LEVEL	Lexile 140
RESPONSE	visualize
VOCABULARY	◇dew ◇high ◇breathe ◇flood
COMPREHENSION	explain
WORD WORK	long *i*
MORE WORD WORK	syllables
WRITING	paragraph

OTHER RESOURCES

The first **four** pages of this teacher's lesson describe Parts I–IV of the lesson. Also included are these **six** blackline masters. Use them to reinforce key elements of the lesson.

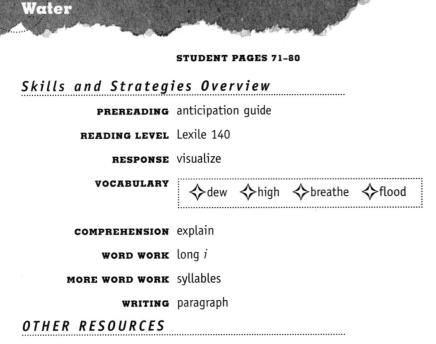

Vocabulary

Prereading

Comprehension

Word Work

More Word Work

Assessment

BEFORE YOU READ

Continue your discussion on water by asking students to close their eyes and notice what they "see" when they think of the word *water*. Do they see water running from a faucet or flowing down a stream? Invite students to share their ideas. Then assign the prereading activity on student book page 72. (Refer to the Strategy Handbook on page 42 for more help on using anticipation guides.)

Motivation Strategy

CONNECTING WITH STUDENTS   Ask students to imagine what would happen if all the water in the world vanished. What do they think would happen to the plants, animals, and people in the world? Help students see how critical water is for all living things.

Words to Know

CONTEXT CLUES   Context clues are one of the most powerful vocabulary strategies for readers. Help students use **context clues** to determine the meaning of some of the more challenging words from *Water*, including *dew, high, breathe,* and *flood*.

To begin, model using context clues by saying: *I see the word* flowing, *but I'm not sure what it means. I'll reread the sentence in which it appears. I'll pay close attention to the words around it that I do know. I know the sentence means something about water moving from the river to the sea. I bet* flowing *is a way of saying that the water is moving.*

Invite student volunteers to try using context clues for other vocabulary words. Then have students complete the **Studying Words** blackline master on page 136.

Prereading Strategies

PREVIEW   For their first prereading activity, students will complete an anticipation guide. First, tell students that there are no right or wrong answers; it is just a way to get them thinking more about water. You might first read aloud the statements and then have students go back and reread them independently. After they complete the activity, have students share their answers with a partner. Make sure they explain why they chose the answer they did. End the activity by coming together as a class and discussing students' ideas.

PREDICT   As a further prereading activity, ask students to make predictions about the selection. Encourage students to begin their predicting by reflecting on the prereading activities they have done so far. Next, have students look over the illustrations and read a sentence or two from the reading. Then ask students to fill out the prediction organizer on the **Before You Read** blackline master on page 137.

MY PURPOSE   Read aloud students' purpose for reading *Water* on the bottom on student book page 72: *What is water and where do we find it?* Point out that students really have two purposes:

1. Find out what water is.

2. Discover where they can find water.

Ask students to keep these two purposes in mind as they read *Water*.

II. READ

Response Strategy

FIRST READING Before students begin their initial reading, explain the purpose of **visualizing**. Direct students' attention to the two "Stop and Draw" boxes that interrupt the text (student book pages 75 and 77). Explain that these boxes are there to help students visualize the events of the story. Point out that to visualize means to create pictures in your mind as you read. Explain that by creating these pictures readers are better able to understand, remember, and enjoy what they read. Ask students to imagine a lake. Have them describe the lake they have thought of. Tell them that visualizing is imagining.

Comprehension Strategy

SECOND READING Have students return to page 74 of their books and review the three steps under Read. Remind them to use this second reading as a means for drawing ideas and facts they want to remember under "My Notes."

Assign the **Comprehension** blackline master on page 138 as a way of furthering students' understanding of the story.

Discussion Questions

COMPREHENSION 1. Where are three places you can find water? *(Answers will vary. Possible: small pond, flood, dew.)*

2. How can water be "high in the sky"? *(Rain clouds are full of water.)*

CRITICAL THINKING 3. What do you think was Frank Asch's purpose for writing *Water*? Why? *(Answers will vary. Possible: I think he wrote it so that everyone realizes how special water is.)*

4. What part of the story did you like best? Why? *(Answers will vary. Possible: I like it when he says "Water is a salty tear" because I never thought of tears as water before.)*

Reread

THIRD READING Invite students to return to the predictions they made about the story on the blackline master on page 137. Have them reread *Water* once more, this time to check their predictions against what really happens in the selection. Have students turn the blackline master over and write a sentence or two about what the story was really about. Invite students to gather in small groups and discuss the relationship between their predictions and what really happened. Remind students that there are no right or wrong predictions; the purpose of predicting is to help readers get more involved in the story by discussing what they thought and why they thought it. You might ask groups how making predictions helped them as they read.

Word Work

LONG I Use the first Word Work lesson on student book page 78 to boost students' understanding of the **long *i* sound**. As a class, brainstorm words that contain long *i*, including: *kite, write, mine, kind,* and *line*. Then check to see if students can differentiate long *i* from other vowel sounds, including short *i*. Ask, *What vowel sound do you hear in* kit? Say *kit* sound by sound. /k/ /ĭ/ /t/. *What sound do you hear in* kite? *What about* tip *and* ripe? When you feel students are ready, assign the Word Work lesson on their own.

Assign the **Word Work** blackline master on page 139 if you feel students need additional practice with long *i*.

More Word Work

SYLLABLES Use the second Word Work lesson on page 79 to offer students practice in **dividing words into syllables.** Walk students through the activity before you have them complete it on their own. First, have students clap the beats to words such as *wet, water,* and *waterfall*. After they clap out each word, note the number of claps (or beats) in each word. Explain that these beats are syllables. Help students see that words with one clap, or beat, such as *wet*, have one syllable, words with two claps, or beats, such as *water*, have two syllables, and so on. Then walk students through the information on the top of page 79. (Note that *water* can be pronounced two ways: wô/ter and wŏt/er.) Once you are sure students have an understanding of how to hear syllables, have them finish the activity on their own.

Assign the **More Word Work** blackline master on page 140 if you feel students need more practice with syllables.

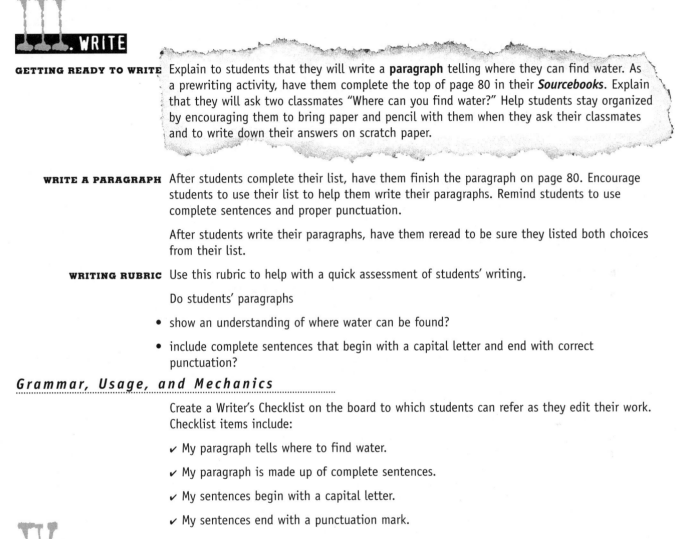

III. WRITE

GETTING READY TO WRITE Explain to students that they will write a **paragraph** telling where they can find water. As a prewriting activity, have them complete the top of page 80 in their *Sourcebooks*. Explain that they will ask two classmates "Where can you find water?" Help students stay organized by encouraging them to bring paper and pencil with them when they ask their classmates and to write down their answers on scratch paper.

WRITE A PARAGRAPH After students complete their list, have them finish the paragraph on page 80. Encourage students to use their list to help them write their paragraphs. Remind students to use complete sentences and proper punctuation.

After students write their paragraphs, have them reread to be sure they listed both choices from their list.

WRITING RUBRIC Use this rubric to help with a quick assessment of students' writing.

Do students' paragraphs

- show an understanding of where water can be found?

- include complete sentences that begin with a capital letter and end with correct punctuation?

Grammar, Usage, and Mechanics

Create a Writer's Checklist on the board to which students can refer as they edit their work. Checklist items include:

✔ My paragraph tells where to find water.

✔ My paragraph is made up of complete sentences.

✔ My sentences begin with a capital letter.

✔ My sentences end with a punctuation mark.

IV. LOOK BACK

End the lesson by discussing the ease or difficulty with which students read *Water*. What parts of the selection did they find easy to read? What parts were more challenging?

To test students' comprehension of the material, use the **Lesson Test** blackline master on page 141.

Name _____

STUDYING WORDS

Before Reading

DIRECTIONS Read each sentence.

Then write what you think the underlined word means.

Use the rest of the sentence to help you.

1. The morning <u>dew</u> made the grass shiny and wet.

I think <u>dew</u> means _____ .

2. The waterfall started <u>high</u> in the mountains.

I think <u>high</u> means _____ .

3. People use their lungs to <u>breathe</u>.

I think <u>breathe</u> means _____ .

4. Streets can <u>flood</u> when it rains too much.

I think <u>flood</u> means _____ .

Practice

Use *flood* in a sentence about a bad storm. Your sentence should give clues about what *flood* means.

Name _____

BEFORE YOU READ

Predictions

DIRECTIONS Read the title of the story. Look at the pictures. Predict what you think the story will be about.

Clue	My Prediction
Clue #1: Title	
Clue #2: Pictures	

Name _____

COMPREHENSION

Double-entry Journal

DIRECTIONS Read the sentences from the story in the left-hand column. Draw what you see in your mind in the right-hand column.

Sentence from *Water*	What I See
"Water is ice and snow."	
"Water is high in the sky."	
"Water is a salty tear."	

Name _____

WORD WORK

Long i Sound

DIRECTIONS Read the words in the word box.

Write the words that have the **long i** sound.

| ship | nice | mile | mill | smile | alive | rib | hide | hid |

Long *i* sound

1. _____

2. _____

3. _____

4. _____

5. _____

DIRECTIONS Choose one of the words you listed on the lines.
Use it in a sentence.

_____

_____

Name _____

MORE WORD WORK

Syllables

DIRECTIONS Read the four sentences.

Underline words with one syllable.

Circle words with two syllables.

1. Water flows down the river.

2. The rainbow came out after the storm.

3. The oceans are made of salt water.

4. What do you know about water?

Practice

DIRECTIONS Use the space below to write two sentences about water.

_____

_____

_____

Name _____

LESSON TEST

Multiple-Choice

DIRECTIONS Write the letter of the best answer for each question on the line.

_____ 1. What does Frank Asch say is deep in the earth?
   A. dirt   C. water
   B. mud   D. fire

_____ 2. Which of these words is not a form of water?
   A. rain   C. ice
   B. heat   D. ocean

_____ 3. How do you think Frank Asch feels about water?
   A. He likes water.   C. He doesn't like water.
   B. He is afraid of water.   D. He likes to swim in water.

_____ 4. What is an important idea in *Water*?

   A. Water is everywhere.   C. People can drink water.
   B. Water tastes good.   D. People swim in water.

Short Answer

What does water mean to you? Write a sentence about it on the lines.

_____

_____

141

Too Many Rabbits

BACKGROUND

In Peggy Parish's timeless favorite, *Too Many Rabbits,* Miss Molly has a problem. Unfortunately, she has allowed a rabbit inside her house to spend the night, only to wake up the next morning to find the box is filled with baby rabbits. Suddenly, it's rabbits here, there, and everywhere as Miss Molly frantically tries to find a good home for them.

Of course, *Too Many Rabbits* is more than the story of rabbits that multiply. It is also a tale of warmth, kindness, and, above all else, compassion for those in need. Parish's favorite theme of kooky chaos and measured madness, personified in her most beloved character, Amelia Bedelia, pervades this book as well.

BIBLIOGRAPHY Students will surely enjoy reading another book by Peggy Parish. These three are written at approximately the same reading level as *Too Many Rabbits:*

(Lexile Beginning Reading)   (Lexile 80)   (Lexile 90)

How to Introduce the Reading

As a warm-up to the reading, have students make predictions about the story using the title as their starting point. Ask: *How many rabbits would you say is too many rabbits? Why?*

Then encourage students to consider what a story about too many rabbits might be about. Have them do a picture walk of the text and use what they see as support for their predictions. Finish your warm-up by asking students to complete the Before You Read activity on page 82.

Other Reading

Children love animal stories. After they finish *Too Many Rabbits,* you might suggest they try one of the following:

(Lexile 90)   (Lexile 90)   (Lexile 90)

Too Many Rabbits

Skills and Strategies Overview

PREREADING	predict
READING LEVEL	Lexile Beginning Reading
RESPONSE	connect with the text
VOCABULARY	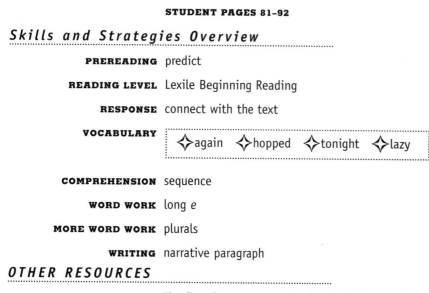

COMPREHENSION	sequence
WORD WORK	long *e*
MORE WORD WORK	plurals
WRITING	narrative paragraph

OTHER RESOURCES

The first **four** pages of this teacher's lesson describe Parts I–IV of the lesson. Also included are these **six** blackline masters. Use them to reinforce key elements of the lesson.

Vocabulary

Prereading

Comprehension

Word Work

More Word Work

Assessment

BEFORE YOU READ

After students complete the introductory activity on page 81, come together as a class and discuss students' lists. Create a master list of things they can tell about rabbits from the picture on page 81. Then direct students to complete another prereading activity—the anticipation guide on student book page 82.

Motivation Strategy

MOTIVATING STUDENTS   Ask students to share their experiences with rabbits. Do any students have rabbits as pets? If so, invite them to talk about the responsibilities involved with taking care of them. You might have students bring the pet rabbits in for a show and tell.

Words to Know

VOCABULARY STRATEGIES   Use the Studying Words activity on student book page 83 to introduce students to regular **plurals**—words that do not change before adding *s* or *es*. Before students complete the activity, walk them through the opening paragraphs. Work with the class to brainstorm other words that follow this same rule. Then have students complete the rest of page 83 on their own.

After students complete the activity, move on to teaching a few key vocabulary words from the selection—*again, hopped, tonight, lazy*. Write the words on the board. Check students' familiarity with these words by asking volunteers to use them in sentences.

If students need additional work with vocabulary, use the **Studying Words** blackline master on page 148.

Prereading Strategies

PREDICT   For their first prereading activity, students complete an anticipation guide to **predict** what the story will be about. Read aloud the directions at the top of student book page 82. Have students read the title and look through the selection to get a sense of what *Too Many Rabbits* is about. Come together as a class and talk about what predictions students can make about the selection. Remind students that making predictions helps them be more active, involved readers.

After the class discussion, have students complete the anticipation guide on the bottom of page 82 independently. Remind them that there are no right or wrong answers; the goal is to build and activate prior knowledge. Make sure you return to the Anticipation Guide after completing the reading and have students modify their answers as necessary.

PICTURE WALK   As an additional prereading activity, have students complete a detailed **picture walk** for *Too Many Rabbits*. Ask students to thumb through the pages of the text, paying special attention to what they learn from each picture and how the pictures make them feel (that is, happy, silly). Then have students complete the **Before You Read** blackline master on page 149. After students complete the activity, encourage volunteers to share their favorite pictures from the selection and explain why they chose them.

MY PURPOSE   Read aloud the purpose statement on the bottom of student book page 82 of the *Sourcebook*. Be sure that students understand that they should use this purpose statement as a guide for reading *Too Many Rabbits*. Return to the purpose at the end of the reading to check students' ability to answer the question successfully.

READ

Response Strategy

FIRST READING Before students begin their initial reading, review their predictions and purpose for reading. Then have students read the selection all the way through, pausing only to complete the Stop and Think activities on student book pages 85, 88, and 89.

Comprehension Strategy

SECOND READING Before students read the selection for the second time, direct their attention to the "My Notes" section on page 84 of the *Sourcebook*. Read aloud the comment one reader made about the text. Explain that the reader was able to make a connection between something in the story and his or her own life. Ask students to note similar connections between the story and their lives as they reread *Too Many Rabbits*. Point out that making these connections helps readers better enjoy and remember what they read.

Discussion Questions

COMPREHENSION 1. What is the title of the selection? *(Too Many Rabbits)*

2. What was Miss Molly's big surprise? *(The rabbit had baby bunnies.)*

CRITICAL THINKING 3. What would you do if you were Miss Molly? *(Answers will vary. Encourage students to explain their responses.)*

4. Why do you think the story is called *Too Many Rabbits*? *(Miss Molly let in one rabbit, but soon there was a bunch of rabbits in her house.)*

5. How would you describe Miss Molly? *(Answers will vary. Possible: kind, caring, likes animals.)*

Reread

THIRD READING To motivate students for a third reading of the text, have them review what they wrote for the Stop and Think activities. Ask students to return to the text and underline words or phrases that support their answers for what happens first, next, and last in the story. Explain that understanding the sequence of events in a story helps readers keep track of key information.

For another way to look at the sequence of events, have students complete the **Storyboard** on the **Comprehension** blackline master on page 150.

Word Work

LONG E Use the first Word Work lesson on student book page 90 to boost students' understanding of the **long *e*** sound. As a class, brainstorm words that contain long *e*, including: *bee*, *mean*, and *queen*. Point out that the long *e* sound is written in different ways: consonant-vowel-consonant (*theme*), ea (*clean*), ee (*feet*), e (*he*), and ie (*field*). Review the list of words students brainstormed. Invite students to categorize their words under *ee*, *ea*, and *other* (such as *ey* as in *monkey*).Then check to see if students can differentiate long *e* from short *e*. Ask, *What sound do you hear in* met? *What sound do you hear in* meet? *What about* set *and* seat? When you feel students are ready, assign the Word Work lesson.

Assign the **Word Work** blackline master on page 151 if you feel students need additional practice with long *e*.

More Word Work

PLURALS Use the second Word Work lesson on student book page 91 to introduce students to a type of irregular plural—those that **change a final *y* to *i* before adding *es*** to make plurals. The crossword puzzle format adds fun to the review.

Assign the **More Word Work** blackline master on page 152 if you feel students need more practice forming these plurals.

WRITE

MAKE A LIST Use the prewriting activity on the top of student book page 92 to help students get ready for their writing assignment. Encourage students to return to the notes they took under Stop and Think on pages 85, 88, and 89, as well as the Storyboard on the **Comprehension** blackline master, to help them remember the sequence of events in *Too Many Rabbits*. Encourage students to be as detailed as possible in their **lists** but to also be sure that they list only the most important events from the beginning, middle, and end of the story.

NARRATIVE PARAGRAPH After students complete their lists, invite them to share in small groups. This is an excellent way for students to be sure they have included the most important events before moving on to the writing assignment. It also offers students an opportunity to defend their choices in the event of any disagreements among group members.

When students are satisfied with their lists, direct them to the writing assignment on the bottom on page 92. Remind them to use their list as a guide when writing their **paragraphs** and to be sure to tell what happens in the correct sequence. End your instructions by talking about what makes a good paragraph. Remind students to begin their paragraphs with a sentence or two describing what happens in the beginning of *Too Many Rabbits*.

After students finish writing, have them reread their work to be sure they've written the story events in the correct sequence.

WRITING RUBRIC Use this rubric to help with a quick assessment of students' writing.

Do students' paragraphs

- tell what happens in the beginning, middle, and end of the story?

- include key events from the story?

- contain complete sentences?

Grammar, Usage, and Mechanics

Before students proofread their work, teach a brief lesson on writing complete sentences. Begin by writing several incomplete sentences on the board. For example:

rabbits in the house   *looked at Miss Molly*   *stayed for a while*

Then ask students what's wrong with these statements. Lead them to see that they are fragments—incomplete sentences that are missing either the subject or predicate (verb). Remind students that a sentence must express a complete thought. Invite student volunteers to turn the fragments on the board into complete sentences. Then have students proofread their paragraphs, paying particular attention to the completeness of their sentences.

IV. LOOK BACK

Reflect with students on their enjoyment of *Too Many Rabbits*. Point out the **Readers' Checklist** and have the class discuss their answers. Explain that these are the kinds of questions good readers ask themselves each time they finish a reading.

To test students' comprehension, use the **Lesson Test** blackline master on page 153.

Name _____

STUDYING WORDS

Before Reading

DIRECTIONS Read the story below.

Tell what you think each underlined word means.

Use the rest of the story to help you.

Once upon a time there lived a <u>lazy</u> bunny. All he wanted to do was sleep. One day he saw a little girl. He <u>hopped</u> over to her. "What a sweet little bunny," said the girl. "Come sleep at my house <u>tonight</u>."

1. I think <u>lazy</u> means _____ .

2. I think <u>hopped</u> means _____ .

3. I think <u>tonight</u> means _____ .

Practice

DIRECTIONS Write a sentence about a time when you were *lazy*.

_____

_____

_____

Name _____

BEFORE YOU READ

Picture Walk

DIRECTIONS Take a picture walk through *Too Many Rabbits*.

Look at every picture.

Then finish the sentences.

My Picture Walk

The pictures make me feel . . .	They make me think about . . .
because	because

My favorite picture is...	I predict *Too Many Rabbits* will be about
because	

Name _____

COMPREHENSION

Storyboard

DIRECTIONS Retell what happens in *Too Many Rabbits*. Draw pictures of what happens. Write a sentence about each picture.

Draw what happens in the **beginning** of the story.

Sentences

Draw what happens in the **middle** of the story.

Draw what happens in the **end** of the story.

Name _____

WORD WORK

Long e Sound

DIRECTIONS Write the word that best completes each sentence.

> bee   beach   eat   street

1. Bunnies like to _____ carrots.

2. Dad got stung by a _____.

3. I look both ways when I cross the _____.

4. We went for a swim at the _____.

Practice

DIRECTIONS Write 4 words from the list that rhyme with *bee*.

> hike   me   hope   three   like   bake   free   see

_____   _____

_____   _____

Name _____

MORE WORD WORK

Plurals

DIRECTIONS Turn the underlined words in each sentence into plurals. Change the *y* to *i* and add *es*.

Write the new word on the line.

1. The three <u>bunny</u> hopped down the path. ___bunnies___

2. We saw lots of <u>puppy</u> at the pet shop. _____

3. There were too many <u>fly</u> at the picnic. _____

4. The twin <u>baby</u> cried all day. _____

5. Our teacher sent the two <u>bully</u> home. _____

Practice

DIRECTIONS Choose one of the plurals above. Use the word in a sentence.

_____

_____

Name _____

LESSON TEST

Multiple-Choice

DIRECTIONS Write the letter of the best answer for each question on the line.

_____ 1. Where did Miss Molly find the rabbit?
A. at the park   C. at her door
B. in her kitchen   D. under a tree

_____ 2. What does the rabbit do when she sees Miss Molly?
A. She hops into the house.
B. She hides in the bushes.
C. She hops away.
D. She bites Miss Molly.

_____ 3. Miss Molly was surprised _____.
A. when she could not find the bunny
B. that the bunny was lazy
C. when she found a box full of bunnies
D. that her cat liked the bunny

_____ 4. Which word below best describes Miss Molly?
A. kind   C. angry
B. silly   D. sad

Short Answer

What would you ask Miss Molly about her life with the rabbits? Write your question on the lines below.

_____

_____

Ronald Morgan Goes to Bat

BACKGROUND

Ronald Morgan Goes to Bat is the story of an enthusiastic, albeit awkward, boy who is determined to win one for the team. When Ronald learns he is going to be on the school baseball team, he is thrilled, even in the face of his classmates' criticism that he "can't hit, he can't catch. He can't do anything." What Ronald does end up doing, however, is far more important: He teaches the other kids that being a team player makes you a winner, no matter how you perform on the field.

In this book and others, Patricia Reilly Giff explores the theme of meeting challenges and facing our flaws. At first, Ronald's teammates laugh at him. Later, however, he earns their respect by figuring out his problem (he closes his eyes while swinging) and finding the best way to solve it. In the end, good humor and camaraderie prevail as Ronald becomes an admired member of the team.

Students who are interested in finding out more about Patricia Reilly Giff and her writing should visit the following website: http://www.edupaperback.org. There they'll find biographical information on Giff as well as her own explanation of how she ended up writing books for children.

BIBLIOGRAPHY Students will surely enjoy reading another book by Patricia Reilly Giff. These three have approximately the same Lexile rating as *Ronald Morgan goes to Bat* (Lexile 200):

(Lexile 190)   (Lexile 210)   (Lexile 210)

How to Introduce the Reading

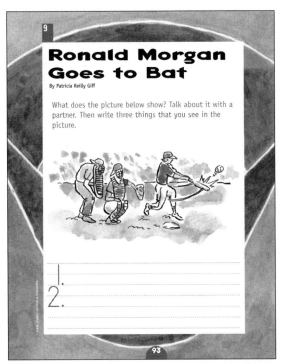

Set the mood for the reading by asking students about their experiences playing a team sport. Ask, *What does it mean to be a "team player"? What happens when teammates don't cheer for one another?* Then brainstorm with students a list of words they associate with "team player." Suggestions might include *enthusiastic, nice, fair,* and *supportive.* This activity will serve as a quick introduction to an important theme in *Ronald Goes to Bat.*

When students are ready to begin the lesson, direct them to read the text at the top of page 93 and then study the picture shown. Point out the lines at the bottom of the page and have students write three things they noticed in the picture.

Other Reading

Set up a classroom library of sports fiction. Have students choose a book to read to themselves or each other. These three titles are particular favorites:

(Lexile 240)

(Lexile 220)

(Lexile 220)

Ronald Morgan Goes to Bat

STUDENT PAGES 93–102

Skills and Strategies Overview

PREREADING	preview
READING LEVEL	Lexile 200
RESPONSE	question
VOCABULARY	✧field ✧practice ✧smacked ✧clutched
COMPREHENSION	retell
WORD WORK	long *o*
MORE WORD WORK	compound words
WRITING	journal entry

OTHER RESOURCES

The first **four** pages of this teacher's lesson describe Parts I–IV of the lesson. Also included are these **six** blackline masters. Use them to reinforce key elements of the lesson.

Vocabulary

Name _____

STUDYING WORDS

Before Reading

DIRECTIONS Read the newspaper article below.

Then say what you think each underlined word means.

Tigers Win Big!

Fans cheered when the Tigers took the <u>field</u> at yesterday's baseball game. Hugo <u>clutched</u> the bat with both hands. The pitcher threw a fastball. Hugo <u>smacked</u> the ball. Home run! The Tigers won! A fan asked Hugo the secret to his great game. Hugo answered, "I <u>practice</u> my hitting every day."

1. I think *field* means _____

2. I think *clutched* means _____

3. I think *smacked* means _____

4. I think *practice* means _____

Practice

Use *practice* in a sentence of your own.

_____

Prereading

Name _____

BEFORE YOU READ

Think-Pair-and-Share

DIRECTIONS Read the sentences below from *Ronald Morgan Goes to Bat.*

Work with a partner. Try to number the sentences in the order you think they will happen in the story.

Then, on your own, make a prediction about the story.

My Think-Pair-and-Share

_____ Then it was time to practice.

_____ But I heard Tom say, "I knew it. Ronald Morgan's the worst."

_____ "I don't hit very well," I said.

_____ Baseball started today. Mr. Spano said everyone could play.

_____ "I hope it doesn't happen again."

What do you think will happen in this story?

_____

_____

_____

Comprehension

Name _____

COMPREHENSION

Story Map

DIRECTIONS Fill in this Story Map about *Ronald Morgan Goes to Bat.* Tell as much as you can about the setting, characters, problem, and how the problem is solved.

Setting

Where does the story take place?	When does the story take place?

Characters

Name two characters from the story.

1. _____ 2. _____

Problem

What is Ronald's problem?

_____

Solution

How does Ronald's teacher try to help him solve his problem?

_____

Word Work

Name _____

WORD WORK

Long o Sound

DIRECTIONS Read the words in the word box.

Write the words that have the *long o* sound on the lines below.

shop slope soap pole dog snow toe tot

Words with Long o Sound

1. _____ 4. _____

2. _____ 5. _____

3. _____

Practice

DIRECTIONS Choose one of the words you listed on the lines. Use it in a sentence.

_____

_____

More Word Work

Name _____

MORE WORD WORK

Compound Words

DIRECTIONS Circle 1 compound word in each sentence from *Ronald Morgan Goes to Bat.*

1. Baseball started today.

2. "He can't do anything."

3. "Stop, everyone," he yelled.

4. Everybody laughed, even me.

Practice

DIRECTIONS Break each compound word into two smaller words.

5. snowflake = _____ + _____

6. classroom = _____ + _____

7. inside = _____ + _____

8. afternoon = _____ + _____

9. sunshine = _____ + _____

10. downstairs = _____ + _____

Assessment

Name _____

LESSON TEST

Multiple-Choice

DIRECTIONS Write the letter of the best answer for each question on the line.

_____ 1. What is Ronald's problem?
A. He can't hit the ball.   C. He can't catch the ball.
B. He quit the team.   D. He got in trouble.

_____ 2. Who tries to help Ronald hit the ball?
A. Tom   C. Michael
B. Miss Tyler   D. his dad

_____ 3. How do you think Ronald felt when the kids laughed at him?
A. silly   C. happy
B. proud   D. sad

_____ 4. Which of the following lessons does Tom need to learn?
A. It is not nice to tease people.
B. You should help people instead of making fun of them.
C. Winning isn't everything.
D. All of the above.

Short Answer

What would you like to say to Tom about how he treated Ronald? Write your ideas on the lines.

_____

_____

1. BEFORE YOU READ

After students complete the introductory activity, come together as a class and have students share their lists. Then have students complete another prereading activity—the Preview Checklist on student book page 94.

Motivation Strategy

MOTIVATING STUDENTS
Tell students that *Ronald Morgan Goes to Bat* involves the game of baseball. Ask student volunteers to share their experiences playing baseball or another team sport. Talk with the class about what it means to be a team player. List their ideas on the board. Ask students to look for more examples of being (or not being) a team player as they read *Ronald Morgan Goes to Bat*.

Studying Words

PAST TENSE
Use the Studying Words activity on student book page 95 to review students' understanding of words with *ed* added. Begin the lesson by talking about the differences between present and **past tense**. Write the following words on the board: *walk, talk,* and *stop*. Lead students to see that these words are all in the present tense—they are about events happening now. Invite volunteers to use the words in sentences. Then explain that adding *ed* to the end of these words turns them into the past tense—things that happened before now. Add *ed* to the words on the board and again have students use them in sentences. Then have students complete the sentences on page 95.

VOCABULARY
Next, move on to the selection's vocabulary. Write the following on the board: *field, practice, smacked, clutched*. Check students' understanding of these words by asking them to use them in sentences. If students need additional work with the selection's vocabulary, have students complete the **Studying Words** blackline master on page 160.

Prereading Strategies

PREVIEW
Students **preview** *Ronald Morgan Goes to Bat* as a prereading activity. Read aloud the directions at the top of student book page 94. Then discuss each item on the Preview Checklist. Ask, *Why is it important to preview the title of a story? Why is it important to look at the pictures?* Then have students begin their preview. Have them check off the items on the Preview Checklist as they thumb through the selection. Then direct students to use their preview to write a prediction about what the story will be about. Invite students to share their predictions in small groups.

For more information on previewing as a prereading strategy, see page 43 of the Strategy Handbook.

THINK-PAIR-AND-SHARE
As a further prereading activity, have students work in pairs to complete the **Think-Pair-and-Share** on the **Before You Read** blackline master on page 161. Think-Pair-and-Share can be a powerful tool for getting students motivated to read, especially for those students who work better in pairs or small groups. Read aloud the directions, and then have partners work together to put the sentences in the correct order. Remind partners that this is a group activity and that both partners should have a say in their answers.

MY PURPOSE
Read aloud students' purpose for reading *Ronald Morgan Goes to Bat* on the bottom of page 94: *Who is Ronald Morgan and what does he do?* Point out that students really have two purposes:

1. Find out who Ronald Morgan is.

2. Determine what he does.

Encourage students to keep these two purposes in mind as they read the selection.

. READ

Response Strategy

FIRST READING Before students begin their initial reading of *Ronald Morgan Goes to Bat*, work with them to review their prereading activities, including the Preview Checklist and Think-Pair-and-Share. Then direct students to read the story all the way through, pausing only to complete the Stop and Retell Activity on student book page 97.

Comprehension Strategy

SECOND READING After students complete their first reading, come together as a class and discuss their initial thoughts about the story. Ask, *What surprised you most about* Ronald Morgan Goes to Bat*?* Then have students prepare to read the selection a second time. Read aloud step 2 on student book page 96. Explain that as students read the story again, they should jot down any questions they have about the story or the characters under "My Notes." Point out the sample question on page 96. Explain that asking questions keeps readers interested in a story.

Discussion Questions

COMPREHENSION 1. Who is Ronald Morgan? *(He is a student who wants to be on the baseball team, even though he isn't a good hitter.)*

2. What happened when Ronald tried to hit the baseball? *(He missed.)*

CRITICAL THINKING 3. Why do you think this story is called *Ronald Morgan Goes to Bat*? *(Because the story is about a boy named Ronald Morgan who wants to be a better baseball player.)*

4. Why do you think Mr. Spano let everyone on the baseball team? *(Answers will vary. Possible: He wants to give everyone a chance to play, even if they are not the best hitters.)*

5. What do you think happens after Ronald's teacher gives him tips for hitting the ball? *(Answers will vary. Encourage students to explain their responses.)*

Reread

THIRD READING Use students' answers to the comprehension questions as a gauge of how well they understood the story from their first two readings. For their third reading, focus on the comprehension strategy of **retelling**. Explain to students that to retell means to tell what happens in the story in their own words. Then have students read the story again to prepare for a retelling. After students read, break into small groups and have students take turns retelling the main events of *Ronald Morgan Goes to Bat*. To help students organize their retellings, have them complete the **Comprehension** blackline master on page 162.

Word Work

LONG O Improve students' phonemic awareness by having them complete the Word Work activity on student book page 100. Read aloud the directions at the top of the page, and then talk about the long *o* sound. Invite students to brainstorm words with the long *o* sound. List them on the board. Say a few sound by sound. Ask, *What are some of the ways long* o *sound can be written?* Help students see that some common ways to write long *o* include *oa* as in *boat* and *ow* as in *slow*. Once you are comfortable with students' understanding of the long *o* sound, have them complete the activity on the rest of page 100.

Assign the **Word Work** blackline master on student book page 163 if you feel students need additional practice with long *o*.

More Word Work

COMPOUND WORDS Use the second Word Work lesson on student book page 101 to review compound words. Invite student volunteers to explain what a compound word is. You might provide hints by writing some compound words on the board, such as *inside*, *bedroom*, and *everyone*. Lead students to see that compound words are made up of two smaller words. Invite students to add other compound words to those listed on the board. Then read aloud the information on the top of page 101, and have students complete the activity on their own.

Assign the **More Word Work** blackline master on page 164 if you feel students need more practice with compound words.

III. WRITE

WORD WEB As a prewriting activity, have students fill in the **word web** for Ronald Morgan on the top of page 102. For students who have difficulty coming up with words to describe Ronald, have them imagine that they are talking about Ronald with a friend. What words would they use to tell their friends about Ronald? Encourage students to use these words in their web.

JOURNAL ENTRY After students complete their word web, explain that they will write a **journal entry** about Ronald. Talk with students about what a journal entry is. Ask students if any of them keep journals or have family members who do. Make clear that journals often are used for writing down people's thoughts and feelings. In this case, students will use a journal entry to write about their feelings for Ronald and what they learned about his character. Remind students to use their Word Web as a guide.

WRITING RUBRIC Use this rubric to help with a quick assessment of students' writing.

Do students' journal entries

- include at least three things that they have learned about Ronald?
- show an understanding of the character?
- include ideas from their webs?

Grammar, Usage, and Mechanics

Create a Writer's Checklist on the board to which students can refer as they edit their work. Checklist items include:

✔ My journal entry tells about Ronald.

✔ My journal entry includes complete sentences.

✔ My sentences begin with a capital letter.

✔ My sentences end with a punctuation mark.

IV. LOOK BACK

Reflect with students on their **enjoyment** of *Ronald Morgan Goes to Bat*. Invite students to name their favorite parts of the story and explain their choices. Would students be interested in reading more about Ronald? Why or why not?

To test students' comprehension of the material, use the **Lesson Test** blackline master on page 165.

Name _____

STUDYING WORDS

Before Reading

DIRECTIONS Read the newspaper article below.

Then say what you think each underlined word means.

Tigers Win Big!

Fans cheered when the Tigers took the <u>field</u> at yesterday's baseball game. Hugo <u>clutched</u> the bat with both hands. The pitcher threw a fastball. Hugo <u>smacked</u> the ball. Home run! The Tigers won! A fan asked Hugo the secret to his great game. Hugo answered, "I <u>practice</u> my hitting every day."

---

1. I think <u>field</u> means

2. I think <u>clutched</u> means

3. I think <u>smacked</u> means

4. I think <u>practice</u> means

Practice

Use *practice* in a sentence of your own.

Name _____

BEFORE YOU READ

Think-Pair-and-Share

DIRECTIONS Read the sentences below from *Ronald Morgan Goes to Bat*.

Work with a partner. Try to number the sentences in the order you think they will happen in the story.

Then, on your own, make a prediction about the story.

My Think-Pair-and-Share

_____ Then it was time to practice.

_____ But I heard Tom say, "I knew it. Ronald Morgan's the worst."

_____ "I don't hit very well," I said.

_____ Baseball started today. Mr. Spano said everyone could play.

_____ "I hope it doesn't happen again."

What do you think will happen in this story?

_____

_____

_____

_____

Name _____

COMPREHENSION

Story Map

DIRECTIONS Fill in this Story Map about *Ronald Morgan Goes to Bat*. Tell as much as you can about the setting, characters, problem, and how the problem is solved.

Setting

Where does the story take place?	When does the story take place?

Characters

Name two characters from the story.

1.   2.

Problem

What is Ronald's problem?

Solution

How does Ronald's teacher try to help him solve his problem?

Name _____

WORD WORK

Long o Sound

DIRECTIONS Read the words in the word box.

Write the words that have the *long o* sound on the lines below.

shop   slope   soap   pole   dog   snow   toe   tot

Words with **Long o** *Sound*

1. _____   4. _____

2. _____   5. _____

3. _____

Practice

DIRECTIONS Choose one of the words you listed on the lines.

Use it in a sentence.

_____

_____

_____

Name _____

MORE WORD WORK

Compound Words

DIRECTIONS Circle 1 compound word in each sentence from *Ronald Morgan Goes to Bat*.

1. Baseball started today.

2. "He can't do anything."

3. "Stop, everyone," he yelled.

4. Everybody laughed, even me.

Practice

DIRECTIONS Break each compound word into two smaller words.

5. snowflake = _____ + _____

6. classroom = _____ + _____

7. inside = _____ + _____

8. afternoon = _____ + _____

9. sunshine = _____ + _____

10. downstairs = _____ + _____

Name _____

LESSON TEST

Multiple-Choice

DIRECTIONS Write the letter of the best answer for each question on the line.

_____ 1. What is Ronald's problem?
A. He can't hit the ball.   C. He can't catch the ball.
B. He quit the team.   D. He got in trouble.

_____ 2. Who tries to help Ronald hit the ball?
A. Tom   C. Michael
B. Miss Tyler   D. his dad

_____ 3. How do you think Ronald felt when the kids laughed at him?
A. silly   C. happy
B. proud   D. sad

_____ 4. Which of the following lessons does Tom need to learn?
A. It is not nice to tease people.
B. You should help people instead of making fun of them.
C. Winning isn't everything.
D. All of the above.

Short Answer

What would you like to say to Tom about how he treated Ronald? Write your ideas on the lines.

_____

_____

The Golly Sisters Go West

BACKGROUND

Students who have never met the Golly sisters are in for a treat with this selection. May-May and Rose Golly—two of children's literature's funniest characters—will charm even your most reluctant readers. Likewise, Betsy Byars's dry descriptions of their escapades will keep students laughing and asking for more.

Before you assign the reading, offer a brief introduction to the book. Explain that the story they're about to read is about two Western showgirls whose greatest joy is to keep themselves and others entertained. Their decision to go West stems from their desire to get back to their singing and dancing "roots" and have a little fun along the way.

Critically acclaimed children's author Betsy Byars has written more than 50 books. Her books have been translated into 19 languages and are enjoyed by children all over the world. Byars has won numerous awards for her writing, including the prestigious Newbery Medal in 1971 for *The Summer of the Swans* and the 1981 American Book Award for *Night Swimmers*. Students who are interested in learning more about Betsy Byars, or reading her writing tips for young authors, can visit her website at www.betsybyars.com.

BIBLIOGRAPHY Students will surely enjoy reading another book by Betsy Byars. These three are all written for younger readers:

ANT PLAYS BEAR

(Lexile 130)

THE JOY BOYS

(Lexile 240)

BEANS ON THE ROOF

(Lexile 280)

How to Introduce the Reading

Ignite students' interest in Byars's text by asking them to brainstorm images that come to mind when they think of the Old West. Students might "see" saloons, cowboys, gunfights, panning for gold, stagecoaches, and so on. Then explain that the story they are about to read is set in a time before there were cars. Ask, *How did people get around before cars and buses? How about before trains and steamboats?*

Next, engage students in a discussion of the advantages and disadvantages of traveling by horse. Ask them to imagine clip-clopping from the East Coast to Missouri or even farther west. Explain: *A trip like that would take weeks and weeks and weeks. How would you feel about sitting in a wagon or walking alongside day after day?* Discuss students' responses. Then assign the first prereading activity on student book page 103. Read the prompt aloud and then direct students to complete the web.

Other Reading

Read aloud or show students the art in other books that relate to the topic of pioneer travel.

AS THE ROADRUNNER RUNS: A FIRST BOOK OF MAPS by Gail Hartman (Lexile 220)

WAGON WHEELS by Barbara Brenner (Lexile 380)

THE JOSEPHINA QUILT STORY by Evelyn Coerr (Lexile 420)

The Golly Sisters Go West

STUDENT PAGES 103–114

Skills and Strategies Overview

PREREADING predict and preview

READING LEVEL Lexile 210

RESPONSE draw

VOCABULARY ◆wagon ◆giddy-up ◆whoa ◆reins

COMPREHENSION sequence

WORD WORK long *a*

MORE WORD WORK adding *ed* and *ing*

WRITING write a note

OTHER RESOURCES

The first *four* pages of this teacher's lesson describe Parts I–IV of the lesson. Also included are these *six* blackline masters. Use them to reinforce key elements of the lesson.

Vocabulary

Prereading

Comprehension

Word Work

More Word Work

Assessment

I. BEFORE YOU READ

To set the mood and give the students some context for the story, continue your discussion of the Old West. Come together as a class and discuss students' webs. Talk about the similarities and differences among students' webs. Then have students complete another prereading activity, Predict and Preview, on *Sourcebook* page 104.

Motivation Strategy

MOTIVATING STUDENTS To motivate students, ask them to predict possible problems the Golly sisters might encounter on their trip out West. You might create a prediction chart to leave on the board throughout the lesson. Invite students to revise their predictions as they learn more about the story. Be sure to review the chart after reading the story to see how closely students' initial predictions match the exact problem.

Words to Know

SILENT LETTERS Use the Studying Words activity on student book page 105 to strengthen students' understanding of *silent letters*. Read aloud the directions at the top of the page. Then invite students to brainstorm other words that have silent letters. Write their ideas on the board. Then have students complete the rest of page 105 on their own.

VOCABULARY Write the following vocabulary words on the board: *wagon, giddy-up, whoa,* and *reins*. Ask, *What do these words have in common?* Help students see that all four words are connected to horses. Invite student volunteers to use each word in a sentence. Then have students complete the *Studying Words* blackline master on page 172. Remind students to use the other words in the sentence to help figure out the meaning of each underlined word.

Prereading Strategies

PREDICT AND PREVIEW As a prereading activity, have students *preview The Golly Sisters Go West* on page 106 of the *Sourcebook*. Invite students to work in pairs to discuss the first question on the page: *What can you learn about the story by reading the title?* Come together as a class and invite partners to share their ideas. Then have students look at the pictures in the story. Remind partners to respect each other's ideas by listening without interrupting. Again, come together as a class and discuss what pairs noticed about the pictures. Then have students use their preview to predict what the story will be about. Alternately, you might work as a whole class to make predictions. Either way, invite students to add or modify the prediction on the class prediction chart.

ANTICIPATION GUIDE Another way to get into a story is through an anticipation guide. Not only does this activity help students make predictions about the text, but it also fosters their ability to follow directions. As you can see from the anticipation guide on the *Before You Read* blackline master (page 173), students have to pay close attention to the directions in order to complete the activity successfully.

MY PURPOSE Read aloud the purpose question on student book page 104. Encourage students to keep this question in mind as they read *The Golly Sisters Go West*.

II. READ

Response Strategy

FIRST READING Review what students know about *The Golly Sisters Go West* before they begin their initial reading. Then direct students to read the selection through to the end. You might have them pause during this reading to complete the Stop and Retell activities, or, depending on your students' needs, you might want to wait until the second or third reading to do so.

Comprehension Strategy

SECOND READING After students read the story through once, come together as a class and discuss what they learned. Ask, *How did the story match your predictions?* Explain that active readers read stories more than once in order to get a better understanding of what they read. Have students read *The Golly Sisters Go West* a second time. This time, have students *draw* what they see in "My Notes." Share the sample sketch on student book page 106. Point out that this is what one reader "saw" when reading the story.

Discussion Questions

COMPREHENSION 1. Where are the Golly sisters going? *(out west)*

2. How were they going to get there? *(by riding a horse and wagon)*

3. What happens when they ask the horse to go? *(He doesn't move.)*

CRITICAL THINKING 4. Do you think the Golly sisters are smart? Why or why not? *(Answers will vary. Possible: I think they are smart because they figure out why their horse won't go.)*

5. What was the funniest part of *The Golly Sisters Go West*? *(Answers will vary.)*

Reread

THIRD READING For the third reading of *The Golly Sisters Go West,* focus on the comprehension skill of *sequence.* If you haven't assigned them yet, now would be an appropriate time for students to complete the Stop and Retell activities on student book pages 107, 109, 110, and 111. As a class, talk about students' responses. Create a sequence chart on the board. Have students help you fill it in, using their Stop and Retell responses as guides. Explain that understanding the order in which things happen helps readers understand and remember what they read.

Use the *Comprehension* blackline master on page 174 as a way of furthering students' understanding of the story.

Word Work

LONG A Use the first Word Work lesson on student book page 112 to boost students' understanding of the long *a* sound. As a class, brainstorm words that contain *long a,* including *tape, made, cake,* and *play.* Say a few of the words sound by sound. Then talk to students about the differences between the short *a* and long *a* sounds. Have student volunteers provide examples of words with either a short or long *a* sound. Have other students determine which vowel sound is used in the word. When you feel students are ready, assign the Word Work lesson.

Assign the *Word Work* blackline master on page 175 for additional practice with long *a.*

More Word Work

SUFFIXES ED AND ING Review what students have learned about suffixes throughout their work in the **Sourcebook.** Remind them that suffixes are word parts found at the end of words. Explain that in this lesson students will learn about the *suffixes **ed** and **ing**.* Invite a volunteer to read aloud the explanation at the top of student book page 113. Help students understand how a word changes when a suffix is added. Ask, *What happens to the meaning of* walk *when I add* ed *to it? What is the difference between* push *and* pushing? Once you have a sense that students understand the notion of adding suffixes, ask them to complete the Word Work activity on student book page 113.

Assign the *More Word Work* blackline master on page 176 if you feel students need more practice with *ed* and *ing*.

III. GET READY TO WRITE

WHO, WHAT, WHEN, WHERE To get students ready for their writing assignment, invite them to complete the prewriting activity on the top of student book page 114. Read aloud the instructions. Spend a minute talking about what students would say if they were going on a trip. Invite student volunteers to share their ideas. Then have students answer the questions *Who? What? Where?* and *When?* Point out that by knowing the answers to these key questions before writing, they will have a head start on their writing assignment.

WRITE A NOTE After students complete the prewriting activity, have a volunteer read aloud the directions for writing a *note*. Remind students that the purpose of their note is to tell about a trip on which they are going (even if it is an imaginary one). Encourage students to refer to their answers from the prewriting section of the lesson as a guide for writing their notes. When students finish writing, have them reread their work to make sure they followed the directions.

After students finish, have them exchange notes with a partner. Post the following Writing Rubric on the board and ask students to assess their partners' notes.

WRITING RUBRIC Have students use this rubric to assess their partners' writing:

Do students' notes

- start with the person they are writing to?

- include when and where they are going?

- tell what they will do on their trip?

Grammar, Usage, and Mechanics

Create a Writer's Checklist on the board to which students can refer as they edit their work. Checklist items include:

✔ My sentences begin with a capital letter.

✔ My sentences end with a punctuation mark.

✔ My sentences tell a complete thought.

✔ Every sentence is about my trip.

IV. LOOK BACK

Reflect with students on how well they were able to read and understand *The Golly Sisters Go West*. If students had trouble following the sequence of events in the story, encourage them to look for clue words, such as *first*, *then*, *next*, and *finally* the next time they read a story.

To test students' comprehension of the material, use the *Lesson Test* blackline master on page 177.

Name _____

STUDYING WORDS

Before Reading

DIRECTIONS Read each sentence.

Then say what you think the underlined word means.

Use the rest of the sentence to help you.

1. The horse pulled the <u>wagon</u> down the dirt path.

I think <u>wagon</u> means _____

2. When I say "<u>Giddy-up</u>!" my horse starts moving.

I think <u>Giddy-up</u> means _____

3. When I say "<u>Whoa</u>!" my horse stops.

I think <u>Whoa</u> means _____

4. Hold on to the <u>reins</u> when you ride a horse so you do not fall off.

I think <u>reins</u> are _____

Practice

Choose one of the underlined words above. Use the word in a sentence to show what it means.

_____

Name _____

BEFORE YOU READ

Anticipation Guide

DIRECTIONS Work with a partner. Number the sentences in the order they appear in the story.

Anticipation Guide: *The Golly Sisters Go West*

_____ May-May said, "Now that we know the right words, we can go west."

_____ "Something is wrong with this horse."

_____ Suddenly, Rose said, "Sister! I just remembered something. There is a horse word for 'go.'"

_____ The Golly sisters sat in their wagon.

_____ They were going west.

What do you predict the story will be about?

_____

_____

_____

_____

Name _____

COMPREHENSION

Problem-Solution Map

DIRECTIONS The Golly sisters had a problem.

Tell about their problem in the left-hand column of this chart.

Tell how they solved their problem on the right.

The Golly Sisters' Problem	How They Solved It

Do you think the Golly sisters did a good job solving their problem? Why or why not?

Name _____

WORD WORK

Long a Sound

DIRECTIONS Read these sentences. Underline the 2 words in each sentence that have a long *a* sound.

1. My aunt Kate likes to snack on cake.

2. Jane came over to my house.

3. Rose and May rode on a trail out West.

4. I petted the horse while he ate hay.

5. My dad gave me ice skates.

Practice

DIRECTIONS Think of 3 words that rhyme with *hay* and have a long *a* sound. Write them on the lines.

Example: clay

1. _____

2. _____

3. _____

Name _____

MORE WORD WORK

Adding ed and ing

DIRECTIONS Add a suffix to each word below. Then write the new word.

1. cry + ing = _____

2. call + ed = _____

3. call + ing = _____

4. plant + ed = _____

5. plant + ing = _____

Practice

Reread the first page of *The Golly Sisters Go West*. Write the word from that page ending with *ing* on the line below.

_____

Use the word in a sentence.

_____

_____

Name _____

LESSON TEST

Multiple-Choice

DIRECTIONS Write the letter of the best answer for each question on the line.

_____ 1. How did the Golly Sisters get the horse to go?
A. They said, "Go!" C. They fed him hay.
B. They gave him D. They said, "Giddy-up!"
a carrot.

_____ 2. What did the sisters ride in?
A. a wagon C. a car
B. a horse D. a truck

_____ 3. How did the Golly Sisters feel when their horse would not go?
A. sad C. happy
B. mad D. tired

_____ 4. How do you think the Golly Sisters felt after they got their horse to go?
A. sad C. proud
B. mad D. tired

Short Answer

What do you think will happen to the Golly Sisters and their horse? Write your idea on the lines.

_____

_____

Stars

BACKGROUND

Stars by Jennifer Dussling makes an excellent launching pad for budding astronomers. In her book, Dussling presents key facts about stars, including their color, size, and shape. Her use of repetitive words makes what could easily be a challenging subject easy enough for even your most reluctant readers.

Before or after they read, your students might benefit from learning about constellations—a topic Dussling touches on but does not explore in detail. Explain to students that a constellation is a group of stars that were imagined to form the shape of objects or creatures in the sky. The majority of the constellations were named by the ancient Greeks. There are 40 constellations recognized today, including:

1. Ursa Major (Great Bear)
2. Leo (the Lion)

Students who are interested in learning more about stars and constellations might visit the following interactive website:

http://www.astro.wisc.edu/~dolan/constellations

BIBLIOGRAPHY Your class may enjoy reading Jennifer Dussling's other books about nature. These three are written at approximately the same reading level as *Stars*:

DINOSAUR EGGS

(Lexile 320)

PLANETS

(Lexile 270)

PINK SNOW AND OTHER WEIRD WEATHER

(Lexile 300)

How to Introduce the Reading

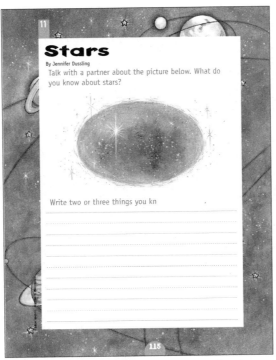

As a warm-up to the selection, ask a volunteer to read aloud the information at the top of page 115. Explain that students are about to read a nonfiction book about stars. Then have students examine the image in the middle of the page and write what they know about the subject on the lines. Tell students not to limit themselves to two or three facts about stars. See if they can generate a long list of information.

When students finish, record their ideas on a sheet of paper that you photocopy for the group. Have students place a check mark beside the facts they can confirm by reading Dussling's book.

Other Reading

Further students' interest in outer space by reading aloud one of the following:

(Lexile 370)

(Lexile 410)

(Lexile 380)

STUDENT PAGES 115–124

Skills and Strategies Overview

PREREADING	anticipation guide
READING LEVEL	Lexile 260
RESPONSE	question
VOCABULARY	✦poked ✦bright ✦grain ✦near
COMPREHENSION	explain
WORD WORK	long *i*
MORE WORD WORK	homophones
WRITING	descriptive paragraph

OTHER RESOURCES

The first **four** pages of this teacher's lesson describe Parts I–IV of the lesson. Also included are these **six** blackline masters. Use them to reinforce key elements of the lesson.

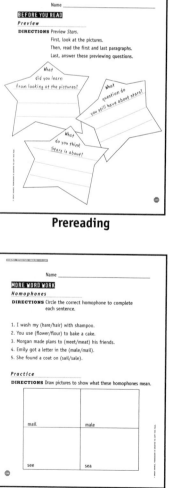

Vocabulary

Prereading

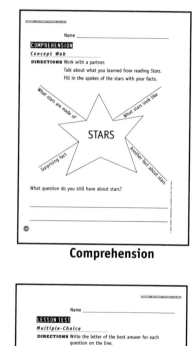

Comprehension

Word Work

More Word Work

Assessment

BEFORE YOU READ

After students complete the introductory activity on page 115, direct them to a second prereading activity—the anticipation guide on page 116. (Refer to the Strategy Handbook on page 42 for more help on using anticipation guides.)

Motivation Strategy

MOTIVATING STUDENTS Review the list of star facts students generated in the introductory activity. Ask students what questions they have about stars. Write their questions on the board. Encourage students to keep these questions in mind as they read *Stars* to see if the selection answers any of them.

Studying Words

ANTONYMS Use the Studying Words activity on student book page 117 as a way of reviewing what students know about **antonyms**. Have students read along as you work your way through the four sample antonym pairs on the top of the page. Invite volunteers to list other antonym pairs. Once you are comfortable with students' understanding of antonyms, have them work in pairs to complete the two activities on page 117.

VOCABULARY After students complete the Studying Words activity, present a brief introduction of some of the key vocabulary words in *Stars*. Write the following words on the board: *poked, bright, grain, near*. Tell students that these are all words found in the selection they are about to read. Ask, *Are you surprised to find these words in a story about stars?* Check students' understanding of these and other challenging words from the selection by asking students to use them in sentences. Reinforce the vocabulary lesson by asking students to think of antonyms for two of the words: *bright* and *near*.

If students need additional work with the selection's vocabulary, use the **Studying Words** blackline master on page 184.

Prereading Strategies

ANTICIPATION GUIDE For their first prereading activity, students will complete an **anticipation guide**. First, tell students that there are no right or wrong answers; the activity is just a way to get them thinking more about stars. You might first read aloud the statements and then have students go back and reread them independently. After they complete the activity, have students share their answers with a partner. Make sure they explain why they chose the answer they did. End the activity by coming together as a class and discussing students' ideas.

PREVIEW As a further prereading activity, ask students to **preview** the selection. Introduce the activity by talking with students about what it means to preview. Be sure students understand that when they preview a selection, they do not read every word. (See page 43 for more information on previewing.) Work with students to create a Preview Checklist, with ideas such as *Read the title*, *Look at the pictures*, and *Read the first paragraph* on it. You might create a master Preview Checklist to photocopy for each student. Encourage students to use their checklist before reading, even when previewing is not an assigned activity. Then have students complete the previewing activity on the **Before You Read** blackline master on page 185.

MY PURPOSE Read aloud students' purpose for reading *Stars* on the bottom of student book page 116: *What are stars? What are some words to describe them?* Point out that students really have two purposes:

1. Find out what stars are.

2. Look for words to describe them.

Encourage students to keep these two purposes in mind as they read *Stars*.

II. READ

Response Strategy

FIRST READING Before students begin their initial reading, review what they have learned about the selection so far. Remind students to keep their purpose for reading in mind as they read the selection as well as the questions they listed earlier in the lesson. Then have students read *Stars* all the way through, pausing only to answer the questions on student book pages 120 and 121.

Comprehension Strategy

SECOND READING Come together as a class and discuss students' initial thoughts about *Stars*. Then read aloud step 2 on student book page 118. Review the sample question under "My Notes." Remind students of the questions they had about *Stars* before reading. Explain that readers often think of more questions as they read. Jotting down questions as they come to mind will keep students motivated to read further. After students complete their second reading, invite volunteers to share some of their questions. Point out that readers will not always find answers to their questions in a selection. Discuss reference sources students can use if they want to find answers to remaining questions, such as websites or other books about stars.

Discussion Questions

COMPREHENSION 1. Is *Stars* fiction or nonfiction? *(nonfiction)*

2. What are stars made of? *(burning gas)*

3. What did people of long ago think the sky was like? *(a bowl)*

CRITICAL THINKING 4. What questions about stars did the selection answer for you? *(Answers will vary.)*

5. What questions do you still have about stars? *(Answers will vary. Be sure student responses relate to the topic.)*

Reread

THIRD READING Use the third reading of the selection as a way to troubleshoot any comprehension problems you identified from the class discussion above. To motivate students for this next reading, have them review what they wrote for the Stop and Explain activity on student book page 120. Ask students to return to the text and underline words or phrases that support their explanations. Point out that when readers can **explain** what they read to others, they will better understand and remember what they read.

For another approach to improving comprehension of the selection, assign the **Comprehension** blackline master on page 186.

Word Work

LONG I Use the first Word Work lesson on student book page 122 to boost students' understanding of the **long i** sound. A long i sounds like its name. As a class, brainstorm words that contain long *i*, including: *sky, spine, night, kind,* and *lie.* Say a few of the words sound by sound. Then read aloud the top of page 122. Ask, *What letter or letters help make the long i sound in these words?* When you feel students are ready, assign the Word Work lesson on their own.

Assign the **Word Work** blackline master on page 187 if you feel students need additional practice with long *i*.

More Word Work

HOMOPHONES Use the second Word Work lesson on student book page 123 to provide practice differentiating **homophones**. Begin the lesson by writing a few homophone pairs on the board, such as *flour/flower, by/buy,* and *meet/meat.* Ask students what they notice about these word pairs. Lead students to see that even though the words sound the same, they have different meanings. Explain that these kinds of word pairs are called *homophones.*

Invite students to brainstorm other homophones to add to the list. Then have students complete the Word Work lesson on their own.

Assign the **More Word Work** blackline master on page 188 if you feel students need more practice with homophones.

WRITE

PLAN Explain to students that their writing assignment for this lesson will be to write a paragraph about stars. Point out that before they write their paragraphs, they will **plan** what their paragraph will include. Talk about the importance of planning. Ask, *How does planning for a trip or a birthday party help you?* Explain that planning before writing a paragraph will help students know what to include in their paragraph and will make the activity much easier to complete. Then assign the top of student book page 124.

WRITE A PARAGRAPH After students complete their plans, have them write a **paragraph** describing stars. Remind them to use their plan as a guide. Encourage students to be as detailed as possible when they write their descriptions. Ask them to imagine that they are writing the paragraph for someone who has never seen a star before. Remind them that a good paragraph includes a topic sentence. They might use the main idea from their plan as a topic sentence, as long as it expresses a complete thought.

After students write their paragraphs, have them stop and think carefully about what they have written. They should ask themselves: *Have I used vivid descriptions of stars? What else could I add to my paragraph to help readers "see" what stars look like?*

WRITING RUBRIC Use this rubric to help with a quick assessment of students' writing.

Do students' paragraphs

• include a topic sentence?

• contain accurate descriptions of stars?

• stay on topic?

Grammar, Usage, and Mechanics

Create a Writer's Checklist on the board to which students can refer as they edit their work. Checklist items include:

✔ I included a topic sentence.

✔ My paragraph includes at least two words that describe stars.

✔ My paragraph is made up of complete sentences.

✔ Every sentence is about stars.

LOOK BACK

Reflect with students on how well they were able to understand the facts presented in *Stars*. Were they able to read it with ease? If not, what did they find most difficult about the selection?

To test students' comprehension of the material, use the **Lesson Test** blackline master on page 189.

Name _____

STUDYING WORDS

Before Reading

DIRECTIONS Read each sentence.

Then say what you think the underlined words mean.

1. The kitten <u>poked</u> at the mouse with his claws.

I think poked means _____ .

2. I wear sunglasses when the sun is too <u>bright</u>.

I think bright means _____ .

3. The wind blew a <u>grain</u> of sand into my eye.

I think grain means _____ .

4. I can walk to school now that I live <u>near</u> it.

I think near means _____ .

Practice

Use *bright* in a sentence about stars.

_____

_____

Name _____

BEFORE YOU READ

Preview

DIRECTIONS Preview *Stars*.

First, look at the pictures.

Then, read the first and last paragraphs.

Last, answer these previewing questions.

What did you learn from looking at the pictures?

What question do you still have about stars?

What do you think Stars is about?

Name _____

COMPREHENSION

Concept Web

DIRECTIONS Work with a partner.

Talk about what you learned from reading *Stars*.

Fill in the spokes of the stars with your facts.

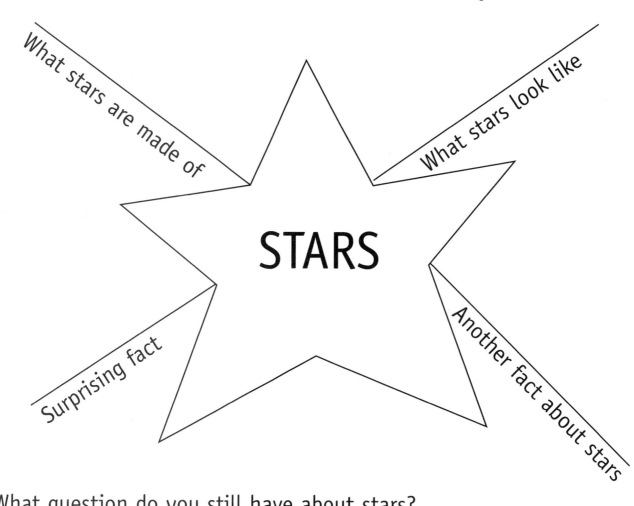

What stars are made of

What stars look like

STARS

Surprising fact

Another fact about stars

What question do you still have about stars?

_____

Name _____

WORD WORK

Long i Sound

DIRECTIONS Read each sentence. Find the missing word in the box. Write the word on the line.

| bright | smile | bike | sky | slice |

1. I had a _____ of bread for breakfast.

2. The _____ sun hurt my eyes.

3. I love to look at the _____ and count the stars.

4. The funny movie made me _____ all day.

5. I hope I get a _____ for my birthday.

Practice

DIRECTIONS Write a sentence about stars. Use a word with the long i sound in your sentence.

_____

_____

_____

Name _____

MORE WORD WORK

Homophones

DIRECTIONS Circle the correct homophone to complete each sentence.

1. I wash my (hare/hair) with shampoo.

2. You use (flower/flour) to bake a cake.

3. Morgan made plans to (meet/meat) his friends.

4. Emily got a letter in the (male/mail).

5. She found a coat on (sail/sale).

Practice

DIRECTIONS Draw pictures to show what these homophones mean.

mail	male
see	sea

Name _____

LESSON TEST

Multiple-Choice

DIRECTIONS Write the letter of the best answer for each question on the line.

_____ 1. A star is a ball of burning _____.
   A. light   C. electricity
   B. gas   D. metal

_____ 2. Stars look small because _____.
   A. they are very tiny   C. Earth is so big
   B. they are far away   D. the moon blocks our view

_____ 3. Which star is closest to Earth?
   A. the sun   C. Mars
   B. the moon   D. the Big Dipper

_____ 4. Which of the following is NOT true about stars?
   A. Stars come in different colors.
   B. Stars are very bright.
   C. Stars are very big.
   D. Stars are very cold.

Short Answer

Why do you think people made up stories about stars? Write your ideas on the lines. Be sure to use complete sentences.

_____

_____

Duckling Days

BACKGROUND

In *Duckling Days,* Karen Wallace provides clear, easy-to-understand information about the lives of a mother duck and her babies. Interestingly, Wallace presents her facts about ducks as a story: "In a nest beside the river a mother duck lays six white eggs." This technique serves an important purpose: to capture and retain the interest of the reader.

If you feel students need some additional information about ducks before they begin reading, you might explain that ducks are relatively small, short-necked, large-billed waterfowl. The following characteristics are true of most species of ducks:

- Males molt (shed feathers seasonally) twice annually.

- Females lay large bunches of smooth-shelled eggs.

- Males and females are differentiated by their plumage and call.

BIBLIOGRAPHY Students might enjoy reading another book by Karen Wallace. Consider suggesting one of the following:

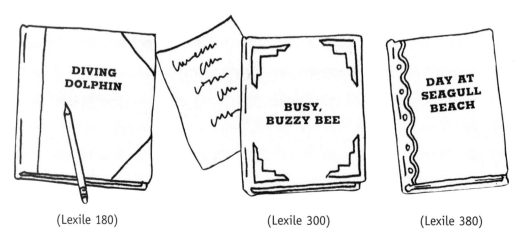

(Lexile 180)   (Lexile 300)   (Lexile 380)

How to Introduce the Reading

Help students make some initial connections to the text by asking them about their personal experiences with ducks. How many have gone to a lake or river and fed bread to ducks? How many have seen them in a park or a zoo or even in their own backyard?

Next, brainstorm a list of duck characteristics. Post your list on the board and encourage students to refer to it as they read. Later, they may want to add characteristics and then use the list to help them complete the writing assignment in Part III.

Other Reading

Continue to foster an interest in nature by asking students to thumb through or read the following:

(Lexile 180)   (Not rated)   (Lexile 360)

Duckling Days

Skills and Strategies Overview

PREREADING	predict and preview
READING LEVEL	Lexile 280
RESPONSE	connect
VOCABULARY	✦gathers ✦downy ✦hatches ✦wobbly
COMPREHENSION	sequence
WORD WORK	short vowels
MORE WORD WORK	adding *y* or *ly*
WRITING	narrative paragraph

OTHER RESOURCES

The first **four** pages of this teacher's lesson describe Parts I–IV of the lesson. Also included are these **six** blackline masters. Use them to reinforce key elements of the lesson.

Name _____

STUDYING WORDS

Before Reading

DIRECTIONS Use the words in the word box to complete each sentence.

    hatches gathers wobbly downy

1. She _____ grass and makes a hollow.

2. She lines her nest with _____ feathers.

3. A duckling _____ from its egg.

4. At first its legs are weak and _____.

Practice

What do you know about baby ducklings? Use 1 or 2 of the words above in a sentence.

_____

_____

_____

Vocabulary

Name _____

BEFORE YOU READ

K-W-L Chart

DIRECTIONS Fill in the K-W-L Chart below.

K What I Know about Baby Ducklings

W What I Want to Know about Baby Ducklings

L What I Learned about Baby Ducklings

Prereading

Name _____

COMPREHENSION

Steps in a Process

DIRECTIONS Tell how a baby duckling hatches.

Put the steps for a ducking to hatch in the correct order. Number each step from 1 to 5.

How a Duckling Hatches

_____ The duckling makes a hole in his shell.

_____ The mother duck builds a nest.

_____ The duckling breaks out of the shell.

_____ The mother duck lays her eggs.

_____ The duckling cracks the shell.

Practice

Now choose one of the steps. Draw a picture of the step in the space below.

Comprehension

Name _____

WORD WORK

Short Vowels

DIRECTIONS Use the words with short vowel sounds to complete each sentence.

    log nest fat fun pick

1. I will _____ the apple. (short i)

2. The bird has a _____. (short e)

3. The _____ hen sat on an egg. (short a)

4. The _____ goes on the fire. (short o)

5. Let's have some _____. (short u)

Practice

DIRECTIONS Write a sentence about baby ducklings using these words. You can add words of your own.

    land duck swim pond

Word Work

Name _____

MORE WORD WORK

Adding y or ly

DIRECTIONS Read the words in each box below.
Make new words by adding *y* or *ly* to the words in the boxes.

New Words

Add y	Add ly
smell silk dirt stick	slow quick nice soft
1.	1.
2.	2.
3.	3.
4.	4.

Practice

DIRECTIONS Now think of two new words on your own that end in *y* or *ly*. Write them below.

More Word Work

Name _____

LESSON TEST

Multiple-Choice

DIRECTIONS Write the letter of the best answer for each question on the line.

_____ 1. What is the first thing the mother duckling does?
A. She builds a nest.   C. She sits on the eggs.
B. She lays the eggs.   D. She cleans the nest.

_____ 2. What is the first thing a duckling does when it is ready to hatch?
A. It makes a hole.   C. It taps and pushes.
B. It cracks the shell.   D. It squeezes out.

_____ 3. The mother duck builds her nest by a _____.
A. river   C. tree
B. mountain   D. bush

_____ 4. Which of the following is NOT true about baby ducklings?
A. Their legs are weak.
B. Their feathers are wet.
C. Their beaks are soft.
D. They stay by their mother.

Short Answer

Why does the mother duckling build her nest near water?

_____

_____

Assessment

BEFORE YOU READ

Direct students' attention to the picture on page 125 of their *Sourcebooks*. Invite students to talk about the illustration. Then have students complete the web independently. Come together as a class and discuss students' webs. Invite volunteers to share their descriptive words. Then direct students to complete another prereading activity—the **predict and preview** on page 126.

Motivation Strategy

MOTIVATING STUDENTS   Review what students know about ducks and ducklings. Then, ask: *What do you want to learn about baby ducklings?* List students' questions on the board. Encourage students to keep their questions in mind as they read *Duckling Days* to see if the selection provides answers.

Words to Know

R-CONTROLLED VOWELS   Use the Studying Words activity on student book page 127 to introduce students to *r-controlled vowels*. Write the following words on the board: *far, cord, germ, bark*. Ask, *What do all these words have in common?* Lead students to see that every word contains the letter *r*. Invite volunteers to say the words aloud. Do students notice anything different about the vowel sounds? Read aloud the top of page 127. Invite students to add other *r*-controlled words. Then have students complete the rest of page 127 on their own.

VOCABULARY   After students complete the activity, move on to teaching a few key vocabulary words from the selection—*gathers, downy, hatches, wobbly*. Write the words on the board. Check students' familiarity with these words by asking volunteers to use them in sentences. Talk about why students think these words would be included in a story about ducklings.

If students need additional work with the selection's vocabulary, use the **Studying Words** blackline master on page 196.

Prereading Strategies

PREDICT AND PREVIEW   For their first prereading activity, students **preview** *Duckling Days* in order to make **predictions** about what the story will be about. Review with students what they have learned about previewing throughout their work in the *Sourcebook*. Talk about the benefits of previewing. Then have students complete the **Before You Read** activity on student book page 126. After students finish their preview, have them gather in small groups to share their predictions.

K-W-L   As an additional prereading activity, you might have students begin the **K-W-L** chart on the **Before You Read** blackline master on page 197. Read aloud the directions to be sure students understand what information to put in each box. Remind them that they will not be able to fill in what they learned until after reading *Duckling Days*.

MY PURPOSE   Read aloud the purpose question on the bottom of page 126 of the *Sourcebook*. Be sure that students understand that they should use this purpose question as a guide for reading *Duckling Days*. Return to the purpose at the end of the reading to check students' ability to answer the question successfully.

II. READ

Response Strategy

FIRST READING Before students begin their initial reading, review their **predictions**, **questions**, and purpose for reading. Then have students read the selection all the way through, pausing only to complete the Stop and Retell activities on student book pages 129, 130, and 131.

Comprehension Strategy

SECOND READING Direct students' attention to the "My Notes" section on page 128 of the *Sourcebook*. Read aloud the comment one reader made about the text. Explain that the reader was able to make a **connection** between something in the story and his or her own life. Ask students to note similar connections between the story and their lives as they reread *Duckling Days*. Point out that making these connections helps readers better enjoy and remember what they read.

Discussion Questions

COMPREHENSION 1. What is the title of the selection? *(Duckling Days)*

2. What does the mother duck use to build her nest? *(grass and feathers)*

3. How do the baby ducklings dry their feathers? *(They stay close to their mother.)*

CRITICAL THINKING 4. Why do you think the story is called *Duckling Days*? *(Answers will vary.)*

5. What was the most interesting fact you learned from reading *Duckling Days*? *(Answers will vary. Possible: I did not know that mother ducks use their feathers to make their nests.)*

Reread

THIRD READING To motivate students for a third reading of the text, have them review what they wrote for the Stop and Retell activities. Ask students to return to the text and underline words or phrases that support their answers for what happens first, next, and last in the story. Explain that understanding the sequence of events in a story helps readers keep track of key information. After students complete this final reading, remind them to return to the K-W-L chart on the blackline master on page 197 and fill in the last box—What I Learned.

For another way to look at sequence of events, have students complete the Steps in a Process activity on the **Comprehension** blackline master on page 198.

Word Work

SHORT VOWELS Use the first Word Work lesson on student book page 132 to review students' understanding of the various **short vowels** explored throughout the *Sourcebook*. Begin by writing the following words on the board: *sat, set, sit, spot*. Ask: *What word contains the short* a *sound? What word contains the short* o *sound? The short* i? *The short* e? Then encourage students to think of additional words with each of these short vowel sounds. Add them to the board until you are satisfied with students' ability to hear the differences among these vowel sounds.

For additional practice, have students complete the **Word Work** blackline master on page 199.

More Word Work

ADDING Y OR LY Use the second Word Work lesson on student book page 133 to provide practice with the **suffixes *y* and *ly*.** Begin by reviewing what students know about suffixes in general. Remind students that a suffix is a word ending that changes the meaning of the base word. Write the following words on the board: *slow* and *smell*. Ask student volunteers to use each in a sentence. Then add *ly* to *slow*. Ask a volunteer to use the new word in a sentence. Discuss how the meaning changes when *ly* is added. Do the same with *smell*. Add *y* and discuss the new word. Then work through the top of page 133 as a whole class.

Assign the **More Word Work** blackline master on page 200 for additional practice.

III. WRITE

Prewriting Strategies

PLAN Use students' responses to the Stop and Retell activities on student book pages 129, 130, and 131 to help them plan their writing assignment. Have students gather in small groups to discuss what happens first, next, and last in the story. Encourage groups to share and compare their responses to the three Stop and Retell activities. Talk about **sequence** clue words, such as *first*, *next*, and *then*. For students having trouble keeping track of the sequence of events in the story, you might have them return to the selection and highlight these and other clue words.

NARRATIVE PARAGRAPH When groups have discussed their responses, read aloud the directions on the top of student book page 134. Then read aloud the directions in each box. Make sure students understand that they are only to write about what happens on the pages listed in each box. As a class, review the pages listed. Make it clear that these pages correspond to the beginning, middle, and end of the story. Encourage students to use their Stop and Retell responses as well as their group discussion as guides for writing their **paragraphs.**

After students finish writing, be sure they've followed the directions in each box.

WRITING RUBRIC Use this rubric to help with a quick assessment of students' writing.

Do students' paragraphs

- tell what happens in the beginning, middle, and end of the story?

- include key events from the story?

- contain complete sentences?

Grammar, Usage, and Mechanics

Before students proofread their work, teach a brief lesson on writing complete sentences. Begin by writing several fragments on the board. For example:

baby ducklings   build her nest   wobbly legs

Then ask students what is wrong with these statements. Lead them to see that they are fragments, or incomplete sentences that are missing either the subject (what the sentence talks about) or verb. Remind students that a sentence must express a complete thought.

IV. LOOK BACK

Finish the lesson by talking about how well students enjoyed *Duckling Days*. Would they be interested in learning more about ducklings? Why or why not?

To test students' comprehension of the material, use the **Lesson Test** blackline master on page 201.

Name _____

STUDYING WORDS

Before Reading

DIRECTIONS Use the words in the word box to complete each sentence.

hatches   gathers   wobbly   downy

1. She _____ grass and makes a hollow.

2. She lines her nest with _____ feathers.

3. A duckling _____ from its egg.

4. At first its legs are weak and _____ .

Practice

What do you know about baby ducklings? Use 1 or 2 of the words above in a sentence.

_____

_____

_____

Name _____

BEFORE YOU READ

K-W-L Chart

DIRECTIONS Fill in the K-W-L Chart below.

K What I Know about Baby Ducklings

W What I Want to Know about Baby Ducklings

L What I Learned about Baby Ducklings

Name _____

COMPREHENSION

Steps in a Process

DIRECTIONS Tell how a baby duckling hatches.

Put the steps for a duckling to hatch in the correct order. Number each step from 1 to 5.

How a Duckling Hatches

_____ The duckling makes a hole in his shell.

_____ The mother duck builds a nest.

_____ The duckling breaks out of the shell.

_____ The mother duck lays her eggs.

_____ The duckling cracks the shell.

Practice

Now choose one of the steps. Draw a picture of the step in the space below.

Name _____

WORD WORK

Short Vowels

DIRECTIONS Use the words with short vowel sounds to complete each sentence.

> log   nest   fat   fun   pick

1. I will _____ the apple. (short i)

2. The bird has a _____. (short e)

3. The _____ hen sat on an egg. (short a)

4. The _____ goes on the fire. (short o)

5. Let's have some _____. (short u)

Practice

DIRECTIONS Write a sentence about baby ducklings using these words. You can add words of your own.

> land   duck   swim   pond

_____

_____

_____

Name _____

MORE WORD WORK

Adding y or ly

DIRECTIONS Read the words in each box below.

Make new words by adding *y* or *ly* to the words in the boxes.

New Words

Add y	Add ly
smell silk dirt stick	slow quick nice soft
1.	1.
2.	2.
3.	3.
4.	4.

Practice

DIRECTIONS Now think of two new words on your own that end in *y* or *ly*. Write them below.

_____   _____

Name _____

LESSON TEST

Multiple-Choice

DIRECTIONS Write the letter of the best answer for each question on the line.

_____ 1. What is the first thing the mother duckling does?
A. She builds a nest.   C. She sits on the eggs.
B. She lays the eggs.   D. She cleans the nest.

_____ 2. What is the first thing a duckling does when it is ready to hatch?
A. It makes a hole.   C. It taps and pushes.
B. It cracks the shell.   D. It squeezes out.

_____ 3. The mother duck builds her nest by a ____.
A. river   C. tree
B. mountain   D. bush

_____ 4. Which of the following is NOT true about baby ducklings?
A. Their legs are weak.
B. Their feathers are wet.
C. Their beaks are soft.
D. They stay by their mother.

Short Answer

Why does the mother duckling build her nest near water?

_____

Clean Your Room, Harvey Moon!

BACKGROUND

Clean Your Room, Harvey Moon! is a funny exaggeration of an all-too-realistic battle between a busy boy and his messy room. Pat Cummings's story, which is told in poetic form, opens with a description of Harvey and his enjoyment of a Saturday morning cartoon. When "the voice of doom" interrupts, however, Harvey must turn off the TV and tackle his messy bedroom.

Throughout the rest of the poem, Harvey cleans and complains, complains and cleans. Thanks to Cummings's sing-song verse and breezy rhythm, however, Harvey's slow, frustrating chore seems interesting, and his moaning and groaning seem funny.

After students finish reading the excerpt in the *Sourcebook*, have them predict what happens after Harvey finishes his room. Later, explain that at the end of the poem, Harvey invites his mother in for a "peek" and learns the unfortunate truth that his mother's definition of "clean" is somewhat different from his own.

BIBLIOGRAPHY Students might enjoy reading another book by Pat Cummings. Here are three of her easiest:

(Lexile 50)   (Lexile 120)   (Lexile 310)

How to Introduce the Reading

Introduce the reading by asking students to think about their own chores at home. Work as a group to generate a list of chores children are expected to do. Items on the list might include: pulling weeds, washing dishes or emptying the dishwasher, taking out the trash, setting the table, and cleaning their room.

Next, have students rank the chores from easiest to hardest or best to worst. Ask also how they'd rank cleaning their room. Is it among the easiest or among the hardest?

Finish the opening lesson by asking students to draw a picture of their room when it gets messy. (See page 135.) Later, invite volunteers to share their work with the class.

Other Reading

Encourage students to enjoy poetry. Work to develop in them a love for the sounds and style of a good poem. Begin the process by reading aloud from one of these modern classics:

(Lexile N/A)   (Lexile N/A)   (Lexile 530)

Clean Your Room, Harvey Moon!

STUDENT PAGES 135–146

Skills and Strategies Overview

PREREADING word web

READING LEVEL Lexile NP

RESPONSE explain

VOCABULARY ✦dirty ✦jumping ✦sweatshirts ✦under ✦dresser

COMPREHENSION retell

WORD WORK long vowel review

MORE WORD WORK contractions

WRITING poem

OTHER RESOURCES

The first **four** pages of this teacher's lesson describe Parts I–IV of the lesson. Also included are these **six** blackline masters. Use them to reinforce key elements of the lesson.

Vocabulary

STUDYING WORDS

Before Reading

DIRECTIONS Read the words in the box.

Count the beats in each word.

Divide each word into two parts by putting a line through the two consonants in the middle.

| sister | pepper | gallop | letter | number |

1. sis/ter

2. _____

3. _____

4. _____

5. _____

Practice

Think of a 2-syllable word with 2 consonants in the middle. Write it on the line. Draw a line between the two syllables.

My 2-syllable word: _____

Prereading

BEFORE YOU READ

Skimming

DIRECTIONS Skim *Clean Your Room, Harvey Moon!*

Let your eyes run down the page.
Watch for words, sentences, and pictures that pop out at you.
Then make some skimming notes.

Skimming Notes

1. Read the first paragraph. What do you learn?

_____

_____

2. List 3 words you noticed.

_____

_____

3. What do you think *Clean Your Room, Harvey Moon!* will be about?

_____

_____

Comprehension

COMPREHENSION

Fiction Organizer

DIRECTIONS Fill in the chart to tell what you know about *Clean Your Room, Harvey Moon!*

| TITLE |
| |

| AUTHOR |
| |

| SETTING |
| Where does the story take place? |

| MAIN CHARACTER |
| Name: |

| PLOT |
| What was the problem and how was it solved? |

Word Work

WORD WORK

Long Vowel Review

DIRECTIONS Use a vowel from the box to complete the words below. Write the word in the right column.

| a | e | i | o |

1. Do you l___ke dogs? | l___ke

2. I want to m___ke cookies. | m___ke

3. She r___de her bike. | r___de

4. Who wants to play on my t___am? | t___am

5. I hope I get h___me before dinner. | h___me

Practice

DIRECTIONS Write 3 new words with long vowel sounds.

6. _____

7. _____

8. _____

More Word Work

MORE WORD WORK

Contractions

DIRECTIONS Rewrite each contraction as two words.

she'd | she would

they'll | _____

won't | _____

we'll | _____

couldn't | _____

didn't | _____

wouldn't | _____

he'd | _____

Practice

DIRECTIONS Write two more contractions on the lines.

_____

_____

Assessment

LESSON TEST

Multiple-Choice

DIRECTIONS Write the letter of the best answer for each question on the line.

_____ 1. Who is Harvey Moon?
A. the author   C. the boy
B. the father   D. the housekeeper

_____ 2. What bothers Harvey most about cleaning his room?
A. He did it last weekend.   C. The room stinks.
B. He had planned to   D. He is missing
   clean it on Sunday.   his TV shows.

_____ 3. How does Harvey clean his room?
A. fast   C. not at all
B. perfectly   D. slowly

_____ 4. Which word best describes Harvey?
A. silly   C. happy
B. complaining   D. crazy

Short Answer

Do you think Harvey's room was messy? Write your ideas on the lines.

_____

_____

_____

I. BEFORE YOU READ

Read aloud to students the introduction at the top of student book page 136. Explain that the selection they're about to read is a poem about a boy who has to clean his room. Ask for comments on the genre of poetry. Do students enjoy poetry, or do they find it intimidating? Then remind the class that one way to get more from a poem—or any type of selection, for that matter—is to try and make a personal connection to the subject the writer describes. In this case, if students think beforehand how they feel about cleaning their rooms, they might find it easier to understand Harvey's reaction to the same task. Follow through on your discussion by assigning the prereading activity on page 136. If you feel students will benefit, brainstorm as a class what they might write in the first box of the word web. Then have them complete the activity on their own. (Refer to the Strategy Handbook on page 44 for more help with word webs.)

Motivation Strategy

MOTIVATING STUDENTS Have students explain how they feel when they're asked to clean their room. Do they moan and complain, or do they try to get it over with in the least amount of time? Then discuss various room-cleaning techniques. Have students offer "advice" to each other on how to clean a bedroom effectively. End the discussion by asking, *If you know you're going to have to clean your room eventually, why don't you do it rather than wait to be told?* Help students see that just about everyone procrastinates when it comes to completing a chore he or she dislikes.

Studying Words

TWO-SYLLABLE WORDS Use the Studying Words activity on student book page 137 as a way to troubleshoot vocabulary problems. After working through the page, you might decide to teach a short vocabulary lesson on forming two-syllable words.

To begin, show students key vocabulary words in *Clean Your Room, Harvey Moon!*: *dirty, jumping, sweatshirts, under,* and *dresser.* Have them work together to divide the words into **syllables**. Remind the class that in most cases, a two-syllable word is divided between the two consonants in the middle of the word. Explain that knowing how to divide a word into syllables can aid in word comprehension, decoding, and pronunciation.

For additional work with the vocabulary words, use the **Studying Words** blackline master on page 208.

Prereading Strategies

WORD WEB As a prereading activity, students are asked to make a **word web** that explores "cleaning your room." As you know, a web like the one on student book page 136 can activate students' prior knowledge about a topic while at the same time encouraging them to make some initial connections between the literature and their own lives. When they've finished, invite students to share their webs with a reading partner. Then post a few webs on the bulletin board and leave them up for the duration of the lesson. Students can refer to them as they read and complete the writing assignment in Part III.

SKIM As an additional prereading activity, have students brainstorm a list of sensory words (words that appeal to the senses of taste, touch, smell, sight, and hearing) that they associate with cleaning their rooms. This quick activity gives students the chance to play with language much the same as a poet does. Invite students to write their sensory words on the **Before You Read** blackline master on page 209.

MY PURPOSE Read aloud the purpose question at the bottom of student book page 136 and be sure students understand that you'd like them to track what occurs when Harvey cleans his room. Encourage students to make notes that relate to their purpose in the "My Notes" columns.

II. READ

Response Strategy

FIRST READING Before students begin their first readings, remind them of the response strategy of asking during-reading **questions.** They should also be able to answer questions a teacher or classmate could pose to them. Tell the class that you'd like them to respond to the questions they see in the "My Notes" section.

Comprehension Strategy

SECOND READING As they read Cummings's poem, students will need to stop at two different points and **retell** the events described. Remind the class that when they retell, they need to use their own words, and not the words of the author. Explain to students that retelling is one way of checking to see that they've understood what they've read. When students have finished, take a look at what they wrote. If you see that some are struggling with the retelling, make note of it. Later, do an oral reading of the poem with these students to see if you can boost comprehension.

For more help with **Comprehension,** assign the blackline master on page 210.

Discussion Questions

COMPREHENSION 1. What is the setting of the poem? *(a Saturday morning inside the house of a boy named Harvey)*

2. What is the voice of "DOOM"? *(It is Harvey's mother telling him that he needs to clean his room.)*

3. What is Harvey's reaction to his mother's request? *(He moans and carries on. He doesn't want to clean his room.)*

CRITICAL THINKING 4. Why is cleaning his room such a challenge for Harvey? *(It's a terrible mess. Also, he would rather watch TV than do a Saturday morning chore.)*

5. What is Harvey's "technique" for cleaning his room? *(Possible: He kind of throws things around and tries to hide the messes rather than clean them up.)*

6. What do you think will happen when Harvey shows his mother his "clean" room? *(Possible: She might think he did a lousy job and ask him to do it again.)*

Reread

THIRD READING Post the following directions on the board:

1. Read for fun.

2. Read to understand.

3. Read to respond.

Explain to students that on a first reading, they should read for enjoyment. On the second, they read to understand what's going on. On the third, they read for meaning—that is, to figure out the author's most important ideas. Then direct students to do a third reading of *Harvey Moon.* Ask: *What is Cummings's message for readers?*

Word Work

LONG VOWEL REVIEW Use the Word Work lesson on student book page 144 as a **long vowel review.** Begin by posting four vowels on the board: *a, e, i, o.* Then ask students to pronounce them and brainstorm words with the same vowel sounds. Make a list of words that students can consult as they complete the activity on page 144.

Assign the **Word Work** blackline master on page 211 if you feel students need more practice with long vowels.

More Word Work

CONTRACTIONS The Word Work lesson on student book page 145 is a review of **contractions**—making them and then changing them back to their original form. Explain to students that in a contraction the apostrophe indicates that one or more letters are missing. For practice, write a series of contractions on the board: *don't, won't, couldn't, she'd,* and *they'll.* Ask students to change the contractions back to the longer form of the words: *do not, will not, could not, she would,* and *they will.* Then assign the activity on the bottom of page 145.

For additional practice, see the **More Word Work** blackline master on page 212.

III. WRITE

WEB To begin, students will complete a **web** that explores their understanding of the character of Harvey Moon. Encourage them to return to the text as necessary to fill in any knowledge gaps. In some cases, the answers they wrote in the "My Notes" sections of the text can help them uncover characteristics of Harvey. If you have time, pull the whole class together for a brainstorming session on Harvey. Duplicate the web on the board and ask for volunteers to write details that apply. Students can refer to the class web as they complete their own. Later, you might ask the class to work together to write a descriptive paragraph about Harvey.

POEM After they finish their webs, students will need to write a **poem** about messy rooms. There are prompts at the bottom of student book page 146 to get them started. Students may choose to use words they wrote in the web. Remind them that poems do not always have to rhyme.

After students finish writing, have them reread their work to be sure they've included descriptive words.

WRITING RUBRIC Use this rubric to help with a quick assessment of students' writing.

Do students' poems

- describe messy rooms?

- contain descriptive words?

Grammar, Usage, and Mechanics

When students are ready to proofread their work, remind them of the characteristics of a poem. Be sure they use capital letters and punctuation correctly. Also remind them of the importance of using an apostrophe in a contraction. If students uncover problems with their poems, they may need to do some rewriting. You might have to support some students by helping them get started with revisions.

IV. LOOK BACK

Reflect with students on the meaning of *Clean Your Room, Harvey Moon!* Were students able to understand Cummings's most important ideas? Were they able to connect the text to their own lives? If not, encourage students to do yet another reading of the poem.

To test students' comprehension, use the **Lesson Test** blackline master on page 213.

Name _____

STUDYING WORDS

Before Reading

DIRECTIONS Read the words in the box.

Count the beats in each word.

Divide each word into two parts by putting a line through the two consonants in the middle.

> sister   pepper   gallop   letter   number

1. sis/ter _____

2. _____

3. _____

4. _____

5. _____

Practice

Think of a 2-syllable word with 2 consonants in the middle. Write it on the line. Draw a line between the two syllables.

My 2-syllable word: _____

Name _____

BEFORE YOU READ

Skimming

DIRECTIONS Skim *Clean Your Room, Harvey Moon!*

Let your eyes run down the page.

Watch for words, sentences, and pictures that pop out at you.

Then make some skimming notes.

Skimming Notes

1. Read the first paragraph. What do you learn?

_____

_____

2. List 3 words you noticed.

_____

_____

3. What do you think *Clean Your Room, Harvey Moon!* will be about?

_____

_____

Name _____

COMPREHENSION

Fiction Organizer

DIRECTIONS Fill in the chart to tell what you know about *Clean Your Room, Harvey Moon!*

TITLE

AUTHOR

SETTING

Where does the story take place?

MAIN CHARACTER

Name:

PLOT

What was the problem and how was it solved?

Name _____

WORD WORK

Long Vowel Review

DIRECTIONS Use a vowel from the box to complete the words below. Write the word in the right column.

a	e	i	o

1. Do you l___ke dogs?	l___ke
2. I want to m___ke cookies.	m___ke
3. She r___de her bike.	r___de
4. Who wants to play on my t___am?	t___am
5. I hope I get h___me before dinner.	h___me

Practice

DIRECTIONS Write 3 new words with long vowel sounds.

6. _____

7. _____

8. _____

Name _____

MORE WORD WORK

Contractions

DIRECTIONS Rewrite each contraction as two words.

she'd   she would

they'll

won't

we'll

couldn't

didn't

wouldn't

he'd

Practice

DIRECTIONS Write two more contractions on the lines.

Name _____

LESSON TEST

Multiple-Choice

DIRECTIONS Write the letter of the best answer for each question on the line.

_____ 1. Who is Harvey Moon?

    A. the author   C. the boy

    B. the father   D. the housekeeper

_____ 2. What bothers Harvey most about cleaning his room?

    A. He did it last weekend.   C. The room stinks.

    B. He had planned to   D. He is missing
        clean it on Sunday.   his TV shows.

_____ 3. How does Harvey clean his room?

    A. fast   C. not at all

    B. perfectly   D. slowly

_____ 4. Which word best describes Harvey?

    A. silly   C. happy

    B. complaining   D. crazy

Short Answer

Do you think Harvey's room was messy? Write your ideas on the lines.

_____

_____

_____

Wilhe'mina Miles After the Stork Night

BACKGROUND

Wilhe'mina Miles After the Stork Night is the story of a little girl (Sugar Plum) who must run through the dark woods to fetch the midwife when her mother goes into labor. Although Sugar Plum is terribly afraid of the dark, she nevertheless races down a "moon-bright road," leaps over gullies crowded with leeches, and crosses a rickety bridge that spans a stream filled with snakes to get Mis' Hattie for her Mama.

The next morning Mis' Hattie tells Sugar Plum to return home to see what the stork brought her. Sugar Plum is delighted with her new baby brother and proud of the role she played in his arrival. The story ends with Sugar Plum's mother telling her that she's old enough to be called from now on by her real name, Wilhe'mina Miles.

Dorothy Carter and Harvey Stevenson first introduced the character Sugar Plum in *Bye, Mis' Lela,* the poignant story of a little girl who must come to terms with the death of her elderly caregiver. Both *Bye, Mis' Lela* and *Wilhe'mina Miles* have earned praise for their lyrical language and sensitive treatment of a bygone era.

BIBLIOGRAPHY Students might enjoy reading another book about bravery. Consider suggesting one of the following:

THE DRINKING GOURD by F. N. Monjo

SACAGAWEA by Jan and Kathleen Thompson Gleiter

BYE, MIS' LELA by Dorothy Carter and Harvey Stevenson

(Lexile 370)   (Lexile 410)   (Lexile 560)

How to Introduce the Reading

14

Wilhe'mina Miles After the Stork Night

By Dorothy Carter

Wilhe'mina Miles is a story about a little girl and her family.

What do you think she and her family will be like? Look at the pictures in the story on page 150. Write three or four words that describe Wilhe'mina.

Miles

Wilhe'mina

147

Have a volunteer read aloud the introduction to the selection on page 147. Then ask students to do a picture walk of *Wilhe'mina Miles* before they make their predictions. As a way of prompting discussion, ask the class:

1. What do you think the story will be about?

2. What do you imagine is the setting?

3. What do you predict will be the main action?

Make note of students' predictions on the board or chart paper so that you can return to them at the end of the unit. Keep in mind that reading to see if a specific prediction comes true can be a good motivator for reluctant readers.

Other Reading

You might want to suggest other critically acclaimed stories written at this same reading level. Here are three possibilities:

FRECKLE JUICE by Judy Blume

(Lexile 370)

IN THE PARK by Lee Huy Voun

(Lexile N/A)

ELSIE TIMES EIGHT by Natalie Babbitt

(Lexile 380)

Wilhe'mina Miles After the Stork Night

Skills and Strategies Overview

PREREADING	preview
READING LEVEL	Lexile 390
RESPONSE	question
VOCABULARY	◇nickname ◇wringing ◇quiver ◇remember ◇moonbeams
COMPREHENSION	explain
WORD WORK	long and short vowels
MORE WORD WORK	syllables
WRITING	friendly letter

OTHER RESOURCES

The first **four** pages of this teacher's lesson describe Parts I–IV of the lesson. Also included are these **six** blackline masters. Use them to reinforce key elements of the lesson.

Vocabulary

Prereading

Comprehension

Word Work

More Word Work

Assessment

▌. BEFORE YOU READ

Read aloud the directions at the top of student book page 148. Explain to students that the selection they're about to read is about a little girl who must help her pregnant mother by running through the dark woods to get the midwife. Then offer additional information on the setting of the story. Explain that it takes place in the bayou region of Louisiana, an area of slow-moving water that is often overgrown with grasses and reeds. After your discussion, ask the class to **preview** the selection. Remind students that a preview can give readers clues about what's to come in a story. Knowing what happens ahead of time can in turn make the story easier to read. Ask students to complete the preview checklist on page 148.

Motivation Strategy

CONNECTING WITH STUDENTS Ask students to reflect upon a time they needed to prove their bravery. What happened? How difficult was it for them to feel brave? What did the experience teach them about themselves and others? After students share their experiences, explain that Sugar Plum, the main character in *Wilhe'mina Miles After the Stork Night* has to muster enough courage to run alone through the woods at night. Encourage students to imagine how they would feel in the same situation. Ask them to make note of their thoughts and feelings in "My Notes."

Studying Words

ADDING ED AND ING Use the Studying Words activity on student book page 149 as a review of *ed* and *ing* endings. Begin by asking: *What happens when you add* ed *to a verb?* (Help students understand that adding *ed* can change a present-tense verb to past tense.) Then discuss what happens when you add *ing* to a verb. List examples on the board, discuss, and then assign the activity at the bottom of page 149.

For vocabulary work, assign the **Studying Words** blackline master on page 220.

Prereading Strategies

PREVIEW Students are asked to complete a **preview** as a warm-up to Carter's story. A preview is a helpful prereading strategy because it gives readers a glimpse of what's to come. Thumbing through the pages they're about to read encourages students to do some initial learning about the subject and can help them anticipate any comprehension problems they might have during their careful readings.

PICTURE WALK As a further prereading activity, have students take a **picture walk** of Carter's story. Explain to the class that during a picture walk, the reader looks at the art or photographs on each page without reading any of the text. As you know, the art that accompanies a selection can provide valuable clues about the topic, tone, and "flavor" of a reading. Students should use the information they've gleaned from their picture walks to make predictions about what will happen in the story.

Use **Before You Read** blackline master on page 221 to support this activity.

MY PURPOSE Read aloud the purpose statement on the bottom of pupil's page 148. Notice that the purpose question forces students to move beyond "read to find out what happens" in order to look for specific information about characterization. Fulfilling this reading purpose will bring students one step closer to a strong understanding of the story.

II. READ

Response Strategy

FIRST READING Before students begin their first readings, explain the response strategy of asking during-reading **questions.** Point out the example in the "My Notes" on page 150. Explain that this is a question that one reader has about the story. Naturally, students will have other questions that they'll want to ask. Each time a question occurs to them, they should make a note of it in the margin. This way they'll be able to discuss their questions after reading.

Comprehension Strategy

SECOND READING At two different points during their reading of Carter's story, students will need to **stop and explain** what has happened up to that point. The Stop and Explain questions in the *Sourcebook* serve two purposes. First, they encourage students to pause and think about the story. Second, they encourage students to self-assess their own understanding of the selection. If the reader finds the Stop and Explain question too difficult, then he or she knows to reread in the area of the question. This can be extremely helpful to struggling readers who have a hard time skimming in search of a single detail.

For more help with **Comprehension,** assign the blackline master on page 222.

Discussion Questions

COMPREHENSION 1. Why is Wilhe'mina sad about her daddy? *(He can't come home to be with the family. He has to stay and work.)*

2. How does Wilhe'mina's mother act when she hears the news about her husband? *(She gets really upset.)*

3. Why does Wilhe'mina argue with her mother when she is told to get Mis' Hattie? *(Wilhe'mina is scared to go into the woods.)*

CRITICAL THINKING 4. Why do you think Wilhe'mina is called "Sugar Plum"? *(Possible: Because she's little and sweet.)*

5. What is Wilhe'mina afraid of? *(Possible: She is afraid to go out at night alone.)*

6. How does Wilhe'mina show her bravery? *(Possible: She runs for Mis' Hattie, even though she is afraid to go out in the dark.)*

Reread

THIRD READING Since *Wilhe'mina Miles* is one of the longer selections in the *Sourcebook,* it may be a good idea for students to complete their third readings as a group. Divide the class into four small groups. Assign one-fourth of the selection to each small group. Have the group read the selection silently and then discuss. When groups have finished, come together as a class to review their work. Post a plot sequence organizer on the board and ask each group to contribute events of the plot. Finish with a discussion of possible themes in Carter's work. Ask: *What's the big idea behind the story?* (theme) *How did the author show it?* (through the plot)

Word Work

LONG AND SHORT VOWELS The Word Work lesson on student book page 157 offers students a review of **long and short vowels** *a, e, i, o* and *u* (short); and *a, e, i,* and *o* (long). Begin by asking volunteers to name the sound each short and long vowel makes. Have other volunteers suggest examples of long and short vowel words. Then direct students' attention to the information at the top of page 157. Read aloud the discussion of long and short vowels. Then assign the activity at the bottom of the page.

For additional practice, see the **Word Work** blackline master on page 223.

More Word Work

DIVIDING WORDS WITH TWO CONSONANTS Use the second Word Work lesson on page 158 to initiate a discussion of dividing words that don't follow exactly the **"divide between the two consonants"** rule. Begin by explaining that some two-syllable words have three consonants in the middle. Suggest that students try to divide the words two ways: between the first consonant and the other two (mon/ster) or between the second and third consonants (pump/kin). Saying the word each way can help students determine which division sounds right.

Assign the **More Word Work** blackline master on page 224 if you feel students need more practice dividing words into syllables.

III. WRITE

PREWRITING On page 159, students are asked to write a friendly letter to Wilhe'mina describing their own family. As a **prewriting** activity, have students make a list of three or more things they'd like to tell Wilhe'mina. Remind that the topic of their letter will be their family. When students have finished, ask: *What are some interesting things you'd like to tell Wilhe'mina? Why did you choose the information you did?*

WRITE A FRIENDLY LETTER After students complete their prewriting work, read aloud the information at the top of student book page 159. Remind the class that their assignment is to write a **friendly letter** in which they describe to Wilhe'mina their own family. Then discuss proper letter-writing form. Explain the location of the date on the page (top right-hand corner), the salutation (Dear Wilhe'mina), and the closing (Your friend . . .). Discuss variations on this form. Then give students plenty of time to prewrite, edit, and proofread their letters.

After students finish writing, have them reread their work to be sure they've included at least three details about their families.

WRITING RUBRIC Use this rubric to help with a quick assessment of students' writing.

Do students' letters

- begin with a salutation and end with a closing?
- contain complete sentences that relate to the topic of family?
- demonstrate an understanding of friendly letters?

Grammar, Usage, and Mechanics

Post a Writer's Checklist on the board and have students use it to proofread their work. Be sure to include the following points:

✔ Have I capitalized every word in my greeting?

✔ Have I capitalized the first word in my closing?

✔ Did I use a comma after my greeting and closing?

IV. LOOK BACK

Reflect with students on their understanding of *Wilhe'mina Miles After the Stork Night*. Ask, *Were there parts of the story you found difficult to read? Why? Do you feel you fully understand the character of Wilhe'mina and the plot of the story?* Direct students who continue to have difficulty with the selection to try rereading it one final time.

To test students' comprehension, use the **Lesson Test** blackline master on page 225.

Name _____

STUDYING WORDS

Before Reading

DIRECTIONS Read the letter.

Use the words in the word box to fill in the blanks.

Use context clues to help you.

nickname   wringing   quiver   remember   moonbeams

Dear Diary,

Today we went night fishing. The moon was very bright. The

_____ made the river look silver. For a long

time, I didn't catch a thing. I was _____ my

hands and worrying. My Daddy said, " _____ ,

this happened the last time." He said my _____

should be "Miss Impatient." Suddenly, my line started to

_____ and shake. I had caught a fish!

Name _____

BEFORE YOU READ

Picture Walk

DIRECTIONS Take a picture walk through *Wilhe'mina Miles After the Stork Night*.

Look at every picture.

Then answer these questions.

My Picture Walk

1. What did you learn about the little girl from the pictures?

_____

2. What did you learn about the time and place of the story?

_____

3. How did the pictures make you feel?

_____

4. What questions do you have about the story?

_____

_____

Name _____

COMPREHENSION
Character Map

DIRECTIONS Use this character map to describe Wilhe'mina. Write what she is like in each box.

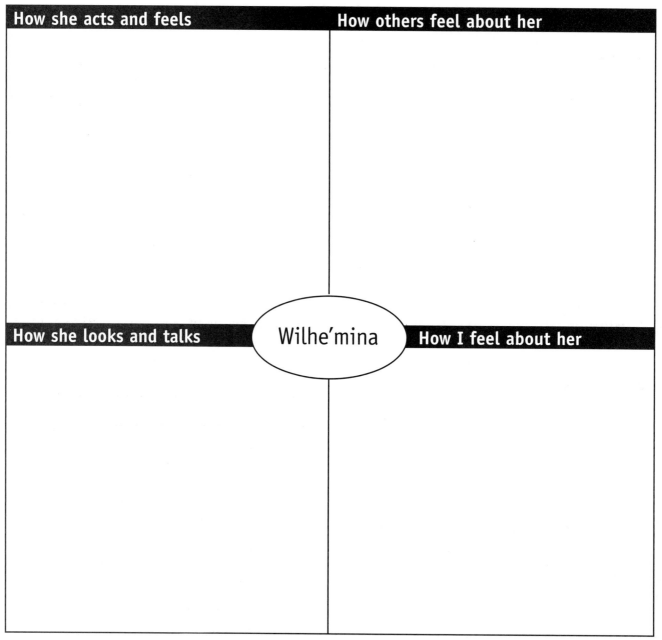

How she acts and feels

How others feel about her

How she looks and talks

Wilhe'mina

How I feel about her

Name _____

WORD WORK

Long and Short Vowels

DIRECTIONS Read the vowels and examples on the chart.
Then add two examples of your own for each vowel.

Long Vowels

a	e	i	o
1. make	feed	like	going
2. _____	_____	_____	_____
3. _____	_____	_____	_____

Short Vowels

a	e	i	o	u
1. cap	hen	pin	top	mug
2. _____	_____	_____	_____	_____
3. _____	_____	_____	_____	_____

Name _____

MORE WORD WORK

Dividing Words with Two or More Consonants

Directions These words have two or more consonants in the middle.

Break each word into syllables.

Say the word, and then draw a line between the consonants to show where the word breaks.

example

1. picnic   pic/nic

2. central

3. hungry

4. picture

5. country

6. common

7. forgive

8. duckling

9. almost

10. dinner

11. follow

12. funny

13. winter

14. outside

15. problem

16. summer

Name _____

LESSON TEST

Multiple-Choice

DIRECTIONS Write the letter of the best answer for each question on the line.

_____ 1. Where does *Wilhe'mina Miles After the Stork Night* take place?
   A. near an ocean
   B. near a city
   C. near the woods
   D. in the suburbs

_____ 2. Why does Wilhe'mina's mother need help?
   A. She can't take care of Wilhe'mina alone.
   B. She is ready to have her baby.
   C. She's upset about Wilhe'mina's father.
   D. She's scared of the dark.

_____ 3. Which word best describes Wilhe'mina?
   A. sad
   B. proud
   C. naughty
   D. courageous

_____ 4. What is an important idea in *Wilhe'mina Miles*?
   A. The woods can hurt you.
   B. It is hard to be alone.
   C. There is bravery in all of us.
   D. Children and adults should get along.

Short Answer

How does Wilhe'mina show that she is brave?

_____

_____

Answer Key

PUPIL'S EDITION ANSWERS
I AM AN APPLE

II. Read

(Students' answers will vary.)

What are two things that have happened to the apple? Use your notes.

(The red bud grew in the sun. It turned into a blossom.)

What did you learn about apples?

(Apples grow from a bud to a blossom to small green apples. Then they turn red.)

Word Work, p. 12

(Students' answers will vary.)

Short *a* sound	Other Sounds
man	his
crack	with
bat	pop
rat	rug
flap	put

More Word Work, p. 13

greenest
sadder
softest
pinker

TEACHER'S GUIDE ANSWERS

Studying Words, p. 64

petal
blossom
bud
stem

❖ petal ❖ stem ❖ bud ❖ blossom

Comprehension, p. 66

1. red bud
2. apple blossom
3. grows bigger

Word Work, p. 67

Students should circle: happy, man, at, bat, hat.

Write the words from the list that have the short *a* sound.

nap
flag
at
rat

More Word Work, p. 68

1. bigg(est)
2. high(er)
3. cold(est)

| 1. tallest | 3. madder |
| 2. darker | 4. slowest |

Assessment, p. 69

1. B
2. D
3. D
4. A

226

© GREAT SOURCE. COPYING IS PROHIBITED.

PUPIL'S EDITION ANSWERS

MICE SQUEAK, WE SPEAK

Studying Words, p. 17

trucks

cars

boxes

dishes

Word Work, p. 22

Short *u* Sound	Other Sounds
cluck	rock
buzz	spot
but	chat

More Word Work, p.23

1. chickens
2. ducks
3. boats
4. frogs

1. wishes
2. foxes
3. kisses
4. boxes

TEACHER'S GUIDE ANSWERS

Studying Words, p. 76

1. Doves
2. crickets
3. owls
4. Coyotes
5. parrots

Comprehension, p. 78

1. baa
2. doves
3. frogs

Word Work, p. 79

1. scr<u>u</u>b
2. t<u>u</u>g
3. p<u>o</u>nd
4. l<u>o</u>ss

5–7. (in any order) tub, pup, mug

More Word Work, p. 80

Left column

1–3. (in any order) rats, bears, fans

Right column

1–3. (in any order) classes, dishes, boxes

Assessment, p. 81

1. C
2. D
3. A
4. B

PUPIL'S EDITION ANSWERS
BREAD, BREAD, BREAD

Studying Words, p. 27
1. trucking
2. picking
3. saying
4. crunching
5. soaking

Word Work, p. 32
1. cap
2. bat
3. man
s@ng
p@t
m@p
s@t

More Word Work, p. 33
skinny, crunchy, lunchy
junky
stuffy
mighty

TEACHER'S GUIDE ANSWERS

Studying Words, p. 88
1. rounding
2. eating
3. growing
4. looking
5. teaching

Comprehension, p. 90
(Students' answers will vary.)
p. 28 bread rolls
p. 29 flat bread and bagels,
       some kind of crunchy bread
p. 30 bread for lunch, pizza, a pretzel

Word Work, p. 91
(Students' answers will vary.)
1. bat
2. can
3. rat
4. fan
5. ram

More Word Work, p. 92
1. sticky
2. cloudy
3. milky
4. hilly
5. dirty

Practice
crunchy
lunchy

Assessment, p. 93
1. D
2. B
3. C
4. C

PUPIL'S EDITION ANSWERS

"SAM'S STORY"

Studying Words, p. 37

he's
she'll
we've

II. Read

(Students' answers will vary.)

Write one thing that has happened so far.

(The rat bought a cat.)

What do you think will happen next?

(The cat will eat the rat.)

What surprised you at the end?

(The cat likes cheese, not rats.)

Word Work, p. 46

(Students should circle the o in each of the words in the top box.)

1. pop
2. job
3. sock

More Word Work, p. 47

helped
wanting
added
calmer

TEACHER'S GUIDE ANSWERS

Studying Words, p. 100

we are → we're
it is → it's
I am → I'm
he will → he'll
she is → she's
they are → they're
that is → that's

Before You Read, p. 101

(Students' answers will vary.)

p. 39 a pet shop
p. 40 a cat
p. 42 He asks what food the cat likes best.
p. 43 He might want to eat the rat.
p. 45 The cat does not want to eat the rat. He likes cheese best too, just like the rat.

Comprehension, p. 102

(Students' answers will vary.)

First, a rat goes for a walk and sees a cat in a shop.

Then, the rat buys the cat for a dime.

After that, the rat and the cat go to the beach.

At the end, the cat tells the rat he likes to eat cheese.

Word Work, p. 103

1. pond   2. soft   3. mob
4. lot   5. clock
6–8. (in any order) mom, sob, top

More Word Work, p. 104

1. keeping   2. owner   3. warmer
4. walked   5. picking

Practice

shining

Assessment, p. 105

1. B
2. D
3. B
4. B

PUPIL'S EDITION ANSWERS
SHOES, SHOES, SHOES

Studying Words, p. 51

shirts
belts
socks
hats
sweaters

Word Work, p. 56

Short *a*
hand
black
Short *e*
pet
red

Short *i*
fit
pin
Short *o*
box
Short *u*
run

More Word Work, p. 57

pens
pets
coats
hands
letters

TEACHER'S GUIDE ANSWERS

Studying Words, p. 112

1. school
2. dancing
3. riding
4. walking
5. ice

Comprehension, p. 114

(Students' answers will vary.)
1. because people have 2 feet
2. old shoes, new shoes, work shoes, play shoes, any-time-of-day shoes, school shoes, dancing shoes, walking and riding shoes, shoes for ice and snow, shoes for sports
3. anywhere in the world
4. Possible: to keep my feet dry
5. Possible: to look good

Word Work, p. 115

1. st<u>a</u>ck
2. r<u>e</u>d
3. r<u>u</u>g
4. s<u>i</u>t
5. b<u>o</u>x

Practice
6–7. (in any order) pin, tag

More Word Work, p. 116

1. bats
2. teams
3. lips
4. pans
5. mugs

Practice
shoes, twos

Assessment, p. 117

1. B
2. D
3. D
4. A

PUPIL'S EDITION ANSWERS

BUILDING A HOUSE

Studying Words, p. 61

(Students should circle the following words in the reading:
bulldozer, bricklayers, fireplace, inside)

II. Read

bulldozer	digs a hole
cement mixer	pours cement
carpenter	puts in windows and doors
bricklayer	builds fireplace and chimney
painter	paints inside and out

Word Work, p. 68

ill	**ig**
drill	big
fill	dig
ip	**ink**
lip	sink
	rink

1–3. (possible answers) hill, digs, big

More Word Work, p. 69

1–3. (possible answers) bulldozer, bricklayers, fireplace, inside

TEACHER'S GUIDE ANSWERS

Studying Words, p. 124

(Students' answers will vary.)
1. person who builds with bricks
2. person who builds with wood
3. person who works with pipes
4. person who works with electrical wiring

Comprehension, p. 126

(Students' answers will vary.)
1. A bulldozer comes and digs a big hole.
2. They hammer and saw. They build the floor, walls, and roof. They put in windows and doors.
3. Painters paint the house.
4. Possible: It takes a lot of people to build a house.

Word Work, p. 127

1. slip
2. miss
3. drip
4. lip
5. little
6. long i

More Word Work, p. 128

2. shortstop
3. inside

Practice
4. stepsister
5. grandmother
6. mailbox
7. fireplace

Assessment, p. 129

1. A
2. D
3. B
4. C

PUPIL'S EDITION ANSWERS
WATER

Studying Words, p. 73

short shorter shortest

big bigger biggest

Word Work, p. 78

nice

pie

spy

high

cry

More Word Work, p. 79

one	two
two	three
three	one

TEACHER'S GUIDE ANSWERS

Studying Words, p. 136

(Students' answers will vary)

1. something wet on the grass
2. far up
3. bring air into your body
4. water covering up dry areas

Word Work, p. 139

1. nice
2. mile
3. smile
4. alive
5. hide

More Word Work, p. 140

1. Water flows down the river.
2. The rainbow came out after the storm.
3. The oceans are made of salt water.
4. What do you know about water?

Assessment, p. 141

1. C
2. B
3. A
4. A

PUPIL'S EDITION ANSWERS
TOO MANY RABBITS

Studying Words, p. 83

rabbits

boxes

kitchens

wishes

II. Read

(Students' answers will vary.)

Write what happens first.

Miss Molly hears a thump at the door.

Write what you think will happen next.

Miss Molly will give away the rabbits.

Write what happens at the end of the story.

Miss Molly keeps the rabbits.

Word Work, p. 90

(Sentences 1, 3, and 4 should have X's.)

What do you do with your eyes?

see

What likes flowers and stings?

bee

More Word Work, p. 91

p	o	n	i	e	s	
			k			
			i			
b	a	b	i	e	s	
			s			

TEACHER'S GUIDE ANSWERS

Studying Words, p. 148

(Students' answers will vary.)

1. not wanting to do work
2. jumped
3. this evening

Word Work, p. 151

1. eat
2. bee
3. street
4. beach

Practice

see

me

free

three

More Word Work, p. 152

2. puppies
3. flies
4. babies
5. bullies

Assessment, p. 153

1. C
2. A
3. C
4. A

PUPIL'S EDITION ANSWERS
RONALD MORGAN GOES TO BAT

TEACHER'S GUIDE ANSWERS

Studying Words, p. 95
asked

laughed

Studying Words, p. 160
(Students' answers will vary.)
1. land used for playing baseball
2. held tightly
3. hit hard
4. to work at something

II. Read
(Students' answers will vary.)

Write what happened in the story so far.
The team practices baseball.

Comprehension, p. 162
(Students' answers will vary.)

Setting	
Where does this story take place? At Ronald's school.	**When does the story take place?** During the day.

Characters
Name two characters from the story. (possible answers) 1. Ronald Morgan 2. Tom 3. Mr. Spano

Problem
What is Ronald's problem? He can't hit a baseball.

Solution
How does Ronald's teacher try to help him solve his problem? She tells Ronald to hit the ball before it hits him.

Word Work, p. 100
rope

go

snow

no

Word Work, p. 163
1. slope
2. soap
3. pole
4. snow
5. toe

More Word Work, p. 101
every   one

any   thing

day   time

More Word Work, p. 164
1. (Baseball) started today.
2. "He can't do (anything.)"
3. "Stop, (everyone,)" he yelled.
4. (Everybody) laughed, even me.

Practice
5. snow + flake
6. class + room
7. in + side
8. after + noon
9. sun + shine
10. down + stairs

Assessment, p. 165
1. A
2. B
3. D
4. D

PUPIL'S EDITION ANSWERS
THE GOLLY SISTERS GO WEST

Studying Words, p. 105

ros(e)
(w)rench
ei(gh)t
(k)not

II. Read
(Students' answers will vary.)

What happens first in the story?
The Golly sisters sit in their wagon to go west.

What has happened so far?
The horse will not go.

What do you think will happen next in the story?
The sisters will say the horse word for stop.

What happens at the end of the story?
The sisters are on their way west.

Word Work, p. 112

Words with Short *a*   **Words with Long *a***
bat   day
dad   bake

More Word Work, p. 113

eating
pulled
showed
growing
telling

TEACHER'S GUIDE ANSWERS

Studying Words, p. 172

(Students' answers will vary.)
1. a cart used to move people and things
2. get going
3. stop
4. straps used to steer a horse

Before You Read, p. 173

5, 3, 4, 1, 2

Comprehension, p. 174

The Golly Sisters' Problem	How They Solved It
They wanted to head west, but their horse wouldn't move.	They figured out the horse words for go and stop.

(Students' answers will vary.)

Word Work, p. 175

1. My aunt Kate likes to snack on cake.
2. Jane came over to my house.
3. Rose and May rode on a trail out west.
4. I petted the horse while he ate hay.
5. My dad gave me ice skates.

More Word Work, p. 176

1. crying
2. called
3. calling
4. planted
5. planting

Practice
going

Assessment, p. 177

1. D
2. A
3. B
4. C

PUPIL'S EDITION ANSWERS
STARS

Studying Words, p. 117
Students should have circled the following pairs of words:

1. play	work
3. dark	light
4. low	high
5. large	small
6. early	late

II. Read
(Students' answers will vary.)

What would you tell a friend about stars?
A star is really burning gas.

What two things can you explain about stars?
Stars are different colors.
The sun is a star.

Word Work, p. 122
Students should circle the following words:
cry, bite, why, right, kite, sight, write, fry, fright

try, like

More Word Work, p. 123
Students should circle the following words:
buy
know
two
four
read

TEACHER'S GUIDE ANSWERS

Studying Words, p. 184
(Students' answers will vary.)
1. to pick at
2. shining
3. a tiny piece
4. close by

Comprehension, p. 186

What stars are made of
burning gas

What stars look like
tiny white dots

STARS

Surprising fact
Stars come in many colors.

Another fact about stars
(Students' answers will vary.)

Word Work, p. 187
1. slice
2. bright
3. sky
4. smile
5. bike

More Word Work, p. 188
1. hair
2. flour
3. meet
4. mail
5. sale

Assessment, p. 189
1. B
2. B
3. A
4. D

PUPIL'S EDITION ANSWERS

DUCKLING DAYS

Studying Words, p. 127

Short Vowels	Vowel Sounds with *r*
man	burn
pig	farm
bug	girl
hen	corn

II. Read

What happens first in the story?
The mother duck builds a nest.
What happens next in the story?
A duckling hatches.
What happens at the end of the story?
Ducklings hatch. They dry out and stand near their mother.

Word Work, p. 132

hat	**win**
tap	with
grass	six
pen	**bug**
shell	fun
nest	duck

More Word Work, p. 133

softly
fuzzy
slowly
dirty
nicely

TEACHER'S GUIDE ANSWERS

Studying Words, p. 196

1. gathers
2. downy
3. hatches
4. wobbly

Comprehension, p. 198

4 The duckling makes a hole in his shell.
1 The mother duck builds a nest.
5 The duckling breaks out of the shell.
2 The mother duck lays her eggs.
3 The duckling cracks the shell.

Word Work, p. 199

1. pick
2. nest
3. fat
4. log
5. fun

More Word Work, p. 200

Left column	Right column
1. smelly	1. slowly
2. silky	2. quickly
3. dirty	3. nicely
4. sticky	4. softly

Assessment, p. 201

1. A
2. B
3. A
4. C

PUPIL'S EDITION ANSWERS

CLEAN YOUR ROOM, HARVEY MOON!

Studying Words, p. 137

dan/cer

drip/ping

pic/ture

ham/mer

hol/low

grab/bing

pil/low

let/ter

short sound

II. Read

(Students' answers will vary.)

What two things have happened in the story so far?

Harvey is watching TV.

Harvey starts to clean.

What are two more things that have happened in the story?

He found his library books.

He put away lots of things.

Word Work, p. 144

long *a*	long *o*
brain	toast
skates	most
long *e*	**long *i***
eat	tie
clean	bike

More Word Work, p. 145

1. he'll
2. she'd
3. wouldn't
4. shouldn't

TEACHER'S GUIDE ANSWERS

Studying Words, p. 208

2. pep/per
3. gal/lop
4. let/ter
5. num/ber

Comprehension, p. 210

Title	*Clean Your Room, Harvey Moon!*
Author	Pat Cummings
Setting	**Where does the story take place?** Harvey's bedroom
Main Character	**Name:** Harvey
Plot	**What was the problem and how was it solved?** Harvey's mom wants him to clean his room. He cleaned it.

Word Work, p. 211

1. l<u>i</u>ke
2. m<u>a</u>ke
3. r<u>o</u>de
4. t<u>ea</u>m
5. h<u>o</u>me

More Word Work, p. 212

2. they will
3. will not
4. we will
5. could not
6. did not
7. would not
8. he had *or* he would

Assessment, p. 213

1. C
2. D
3. D
4. B

PUPIL'S EDITION ANSWERS

WILHE'MINA MILES AFTER THE STORK NIGHT

Studying Words, p. 149

1. coming
2. holding
3. shaking
4. promised
5. crossing

II. Read

What did the letter say?

Sugar Plum's daddy is not coming home.

Write what you think will happen next.

(Students' answers will vary.)

Sugar Plum will get someone to help her Mama.

Word Work, p. 157

Short Vowel Sounds	Long Vowel Sounds
run	bite
fish	cry
got	home
catch	brave

More Word Work, p. 158

bas/ket
tad/pole
mat/ter
sum/mer
soc/cer
Dad/dy
Sun/day
les/son

TEACHER'S GUIDE ANSWERS

Studying Words, p. 220

Words should appear in this order:

moonbeams

wringing

Remember

nickname

quiver

Comprehension, p. 222

How she acts and feels	How others feel about her
She cares about her mom and dad.	Her mom says she's brave and smart.
How she looks and talks	How I feel about her
She's cute. She has pigtails. She's nice to her mom.	She's brave and nice.

(center: Wilhe'mina)

Word Work, p. 223

(Students' answers will vary.)

2. take need bike slow
3. rake seed hike low

2. rap pen win stop hug
3. hat hen spin hop bug

More Word Work, p. 224

1. pic/nic
2. mis/take
3. hun/gry
4. pic/ture
5. coun/try
6. fright/en
7. for/give
8. duck/ling
9. al/most
10. din/ner
11. fol/low
12. fun/ny
13. win/ter
14. out/side
15. prob/lem
16. sum/mer

Assessment, p. 225

1. C
2. B
3. D
4. C

Index

PE signals a pupil's edition page number.

TG signals a teacher's guide page number.